How Hockey Happened

A Pictorial History of the Origins of Canada's National Winter Game

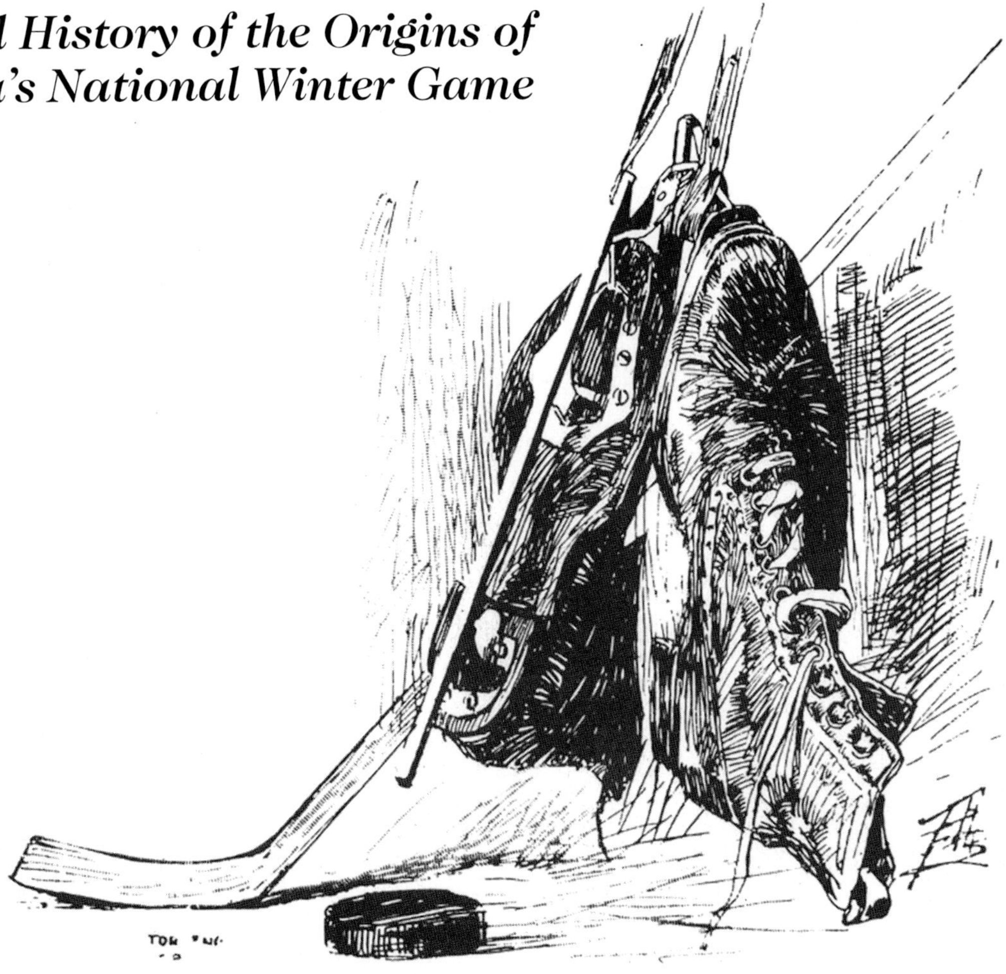

How Hockey Happened

A Pictorial History of the Origins of Canada's National Winter Game

J.W. (Bill) Fitsell

Left: Artist E.C. Coates captures the rousing action of North American aboriginals playing lacrosse on an icy bay in 1859

Dedication: To those hockey aficionados who save, preserve, explore, study, analyze, interpret, and promote the game's history ...

The publisher acknowledges the support of the Book Publishing Industry Development Program of the Department of Canadian Heritage.

Canadian Cataloguing in Publication Data available.

ISBN 1-55082-347-7

Edited by Bob Hilderley.
Designed and typeset by Laura Brady.
Printed and bound in Canada by Tri-Graphic Printing, Ottawa, Ontario.

Published by Quarry Press Inc,
P.O. Box 1061, Kingston, Ontario K7N 4Y5.

The history of hockey meets the future of hockey.

Table of Contents

Foreword

Hockey's Boswell

Each major sport has its James Boswell, a biographer who traces its often serpentine history and comments on its multifaceted features, past and present. Doubtless, hockey's Boswell is John Walter (Bill) Fitsell. He is hockey's historian par excellence.

Drawing on five decades of extensive, voluminous research, Bill has already written two books on hockey (*Hockey's Captains, Colonels & Kings* in 1987 and *Hockey's Hub: Three Centuries of Hockey in Kingston* in 2003), plus innumerable articles published in newspapers, journals, and books that have focused on the origins and development of the game. His meticulous and painstaking research has led him to scour numerous archives, libraries, and collections of private papers across Canada and the northeastern United States.

In *How Hockey Happened*, his guiding research principle remains an unswerving adherence to accuracy and fidelity to facts, irrespective of the impact it may have on a variety of personal sensitivities and sociopolitical interests. Setting aside previously received wisdom on hockey's origins, Bill has burrowed deep inside this colorful universe of research, emerging with valuable factual nuggets, insightful interpretations, and fresh perspectives on the history of hockey, such that anyone venturing in his contentious sphere of study must seriously come to grips with his empirical findings and cogent arguments. There is very little that he has overlooked or not encountered in the realm of early hockey history.

In this book, Bill summarizes the 'origin' debate succinctly and authoritatively, something hockey historians and fans of all stripes need at this juncture of the debate. He examines the roots of hockey as we now know it by considering the role various stick and ball games, many with British-Irish

Cherubs jousting with stick and ball represent the antiquity of hockey-like games.

pedigree (such as hurling, shinty, bandy, and field hockey) and some indigenous North American games (such as gughawat, lacrosse, shinny, rickets, and ice polo) have played in hockey's development. He demonstrates how specific elements of these games were integrated with ice-skating by enterprising nineteenth-century sport enthusiasts to form, quite unexpectedly, a unique hybrid game now simply called hockey. One of the many virtues of this book is that the author has gone as far as anyone can with the available evidence to assay the contributions made to the development of hockey by other team games in the British Isles and Canada. Another virtue is Bill's enthusiasm for the game, which shines through in everything he writes.

Edward R. Grenda
Vice President
Society for International Hockey Research

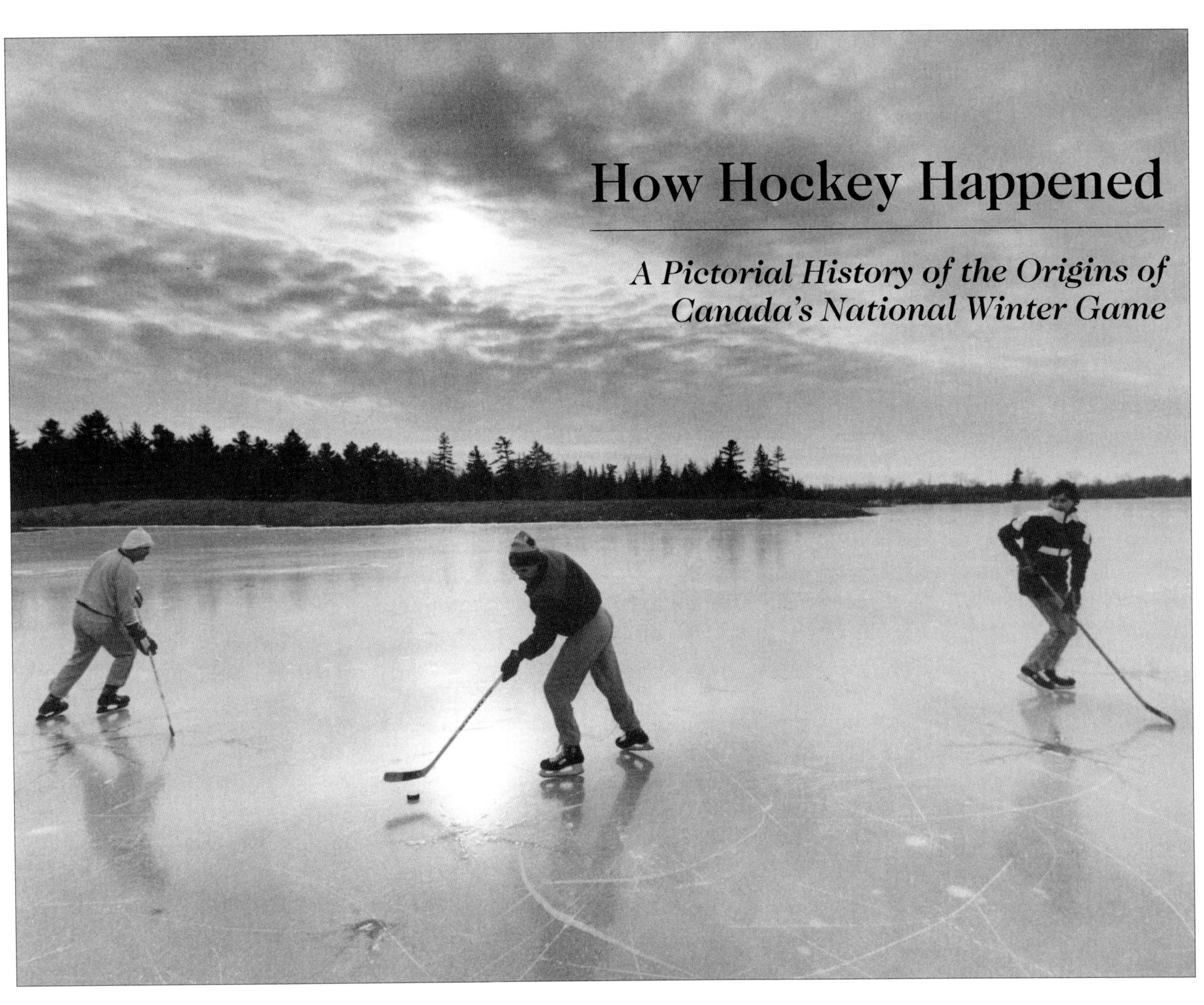
How Hockey Happened
A Pictorial History of the Origins of Canada's National Winter Game

"What a smashing game you Canadians have invented!"

— The Queen Mother (Rita McGrattan)
in the play, *The Queen and I*,
Grand Theatre, Kingston, 1996

Introduction

What a smashing game . . .

What is hockey? Few Canadians think they need to ask themselves this question. Most are convinced they know what hockey *is*. They are also quite aware of what the game *means* to them. But few Canadians have heard about the origins of the game – where it came from, how it started, and what contributed to its makeup? Battles rage among pretenders to the birthplace of hockey, but the parents and ancestors of this rough and ready child are not well known.

Challenged by the question of hockey's genesis, students of the game might turn to encyclopedias and the Internet for help, and find there a mountain of information, much of it equivocal, some of it conflicting, a lot of it flawed because of inadequate research.

"The game of ice hockey originated in Canada, but the place and the persons responsible for its introduction are unknown," we learn from *Collier's Encyclopedia* (1966). *Merit Students Encyclopedia* (1967) doesn't offer much more help: "The origin of ice hockey is obscure. Historians generally agree that it was first played in Halifax, Montreal or Kingston." In the *New York Times* (1947), a reporter admits: "Origins of few sports are so surrounded in mystery as those of ice hockey — a thoroughly modern game."

If the origins of the game appear to be a mystery, claims to its birthplace have become a long-running controversy. In a Kingston hockey program in 1933, the claim is made for the one-time capital of the United Province of Canada as being the first home of our national winter game: "From the time the first game of hockey in the world was played on the harbour ice, Kingston has been noted as the real home of the sport." By 1950, this claim had become a 'fact' in the *Columbia Encyclopedia*: "The first ice hockey

When Dutch sportsmen on skates crossed sticks in this 17th century painting, the ice game was an individual contest that developed into golf.

This warrior-like Dutchman donned skates to play "kolf." Note the two balls and the long stick in the style of a golf club.

league was formed in Kingston in 1885." This erroneous claim was perpetuated in an entry in *Sport International* a decade later: "1860: First recorded 'proper' game played at Kingston, Ont." In 1971, the *Encyclopedia Americana* followed suit, but backed up the date of the first 'proper' game by five years: "The first organized game was played in Kingston, Ont. in 1855."

While these encyclopedia entries seemed to be decisive, they actually proved to be divisive, rejected by hockey historians and even novelists in Halifax and Montreal. "Ice hockey, Canada's national game, began on the Dartmouth Lakes in the eighteenth century," wrote celebrated Nova Scotia author Thomas H. Raddall in *Halifax — Warden of the North* (1948). "The Canadian-born sport was first played at Halifax, where in its Neanderthal days, players used a round puck and strapped blades on their shoes," stated the *Pictorial History of American Sports* in 1952. This claim has been repeated many times since then. Fellow hockey fans from Windsor would later claim that small town in the Annapolis Valley as the birthplace of hockey.

Kingston, Montreal, and Halifax are not the only contenders for this honour. "The game was probably standardized by the students of McGill University in the 1870s," we read in the *Columbia University Encyclopedia* (1950). Maritimer J.G.A. Creighton is credited with establishing a version of the first rudimentary of rules for indoor hockey when he moved to Montreal. In a clipping from

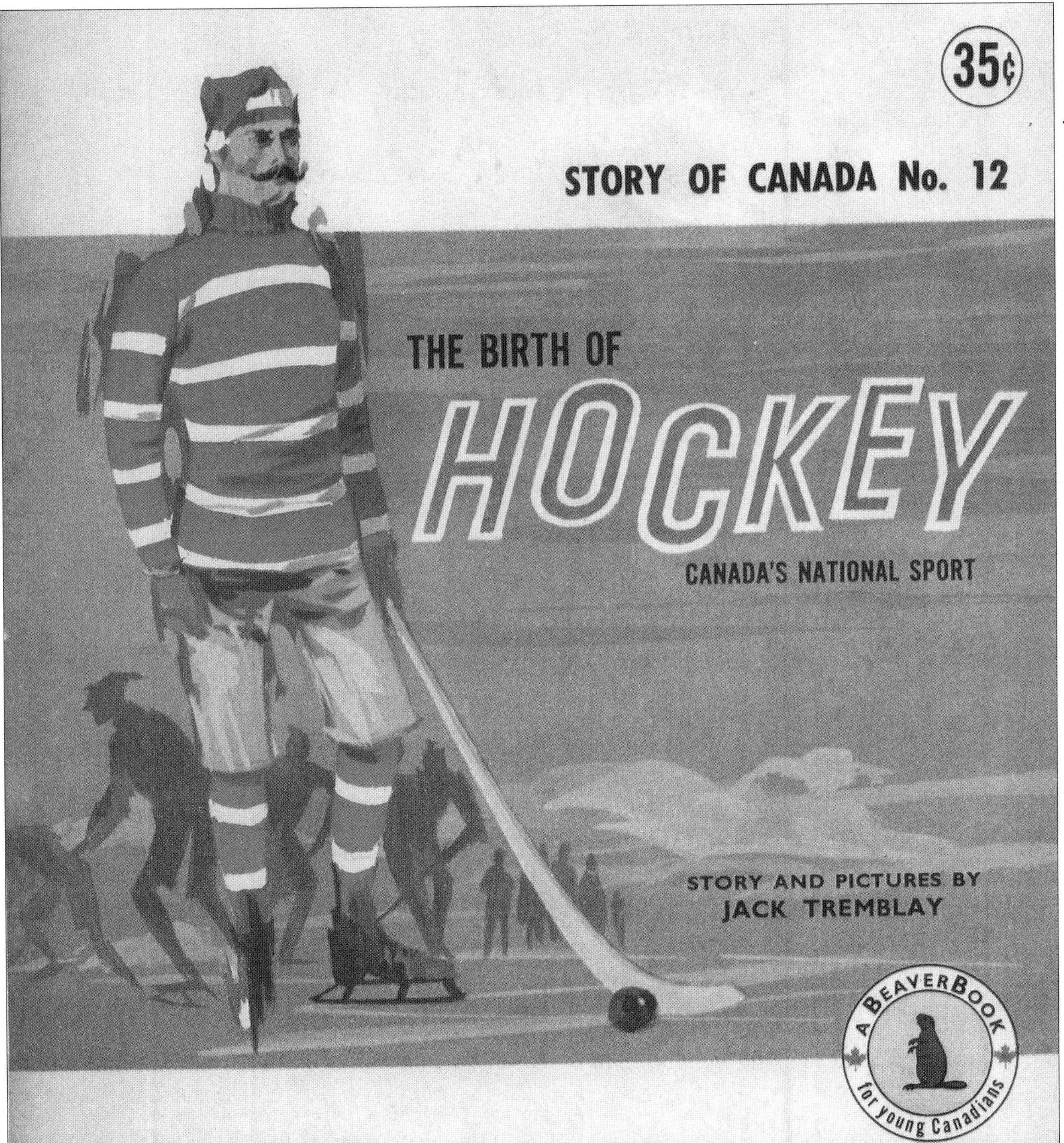

In 1967, Centennial Year, New Brunswicker Jack Tremblay was the first artist-writer to portray hockey's birth and colourful development.

the *Old McGill* newspaper in 1906, we read that hockey "was invented less than 20 years ago by some students of McGill University in Montreal." Ottawa's Clem Beauchamp, one of the nation's unsung hockey historians, supported this birth claim in *The Montreal Star* in 1942: "Hockey as played in Canada ... is a distinctly Canadian developed sport, which was adopted universally after its birth in Montreal as the standard, competitive team game on ice."

Still, there was enough uncertainty about the birthplace of hockey in 1962 that the *Encyclopedia Canadian* threw up its arms and arrived at a typically Canadian fence-sitting position on this question: "But in whatever town or city the game was born, there is no doubt that it developed in Canada."

The *Sports Dictionary* on the Internet offers another tack on this the question in an entry on the origins of North America's four premier sports by declaring their inventors:

Inventor of Basketball: James Naismith
Inventor of Football: Walter Camp
Inventor of Baseball: Abner Doubleday
Inventor of Hockey: J.G.A. Creighton

Creighton and his Montreal mates in 1873 might have standardized hockey's playing area by moving the game indoors, in contrast to the pastimes of ricket and shinny, with their undefined

Looking like a Dutch master, this bare-handed player propels a ball in a modern-day creation by American artist Jacobson.

In this 1970 cartoon, Dunn & Scaduto have fun with the legend that Kingston is the birthplace of hockey. British troops are alleged to have cleared the ice at Fort Frontenac (Tete du Pont) Barracks and played a version of field hockey on the harbour ice in 1861. Other historians have claimed the Ontario city created the game as early as 1843 or 1855. However, the first organized game was not recorded in Kingston until 1886.

outdoor ice surfaces. The confined rink spaces also necessitated the reduction in the number of players, leading to nine-man, then seven-man, and eventually six-man teams. But hockey wasn't born in a blinding flash of an inventor's genius, as was basketball in the imagination of Canadian James Naismith in the 1890s. "Hockey was no brainchild conceived in the night and put into practice the next day," McGill University official E.M. Orlick opined in the *McGill News* (1943). "The question is not when the game of field hockey, hoquet, hurling or shinney started, but rather when and where did hurley or shinney develop into the game of ice hockey as we know it today?"

Despite many seemingly authoritative comments on the origins of hockey and disputes about its birthplace of hockey, the ultimate truth is that hockey, the great Canadian ice game, was not born, invented, or created — it just happened. Hockey evolved from several pastimes played on both land and ice in different parts of the northern hemisphere and developed into the thrilling and sometimes brutal sport that most of the world knows today. As celebrated historian A.M. Lower commented in *Canada – A Nation* (1948), "There is no proof as to where and how hockey originated, but its chief ancestors seem to have been shinny and field hockey." Looking for the ancestors of hockey might prove a more fruitful approach than looking for inventors and birthplaces. "No game or sport comes into being from a standing start," Robert Giddens remarked in his book, *Ice Hockey*. "There are always traces of old sport in the new."

So, to discover hockey's roots, let's inspect its various predecessors, such games as hurling in Ireland, shinty in Scotland, bandy and field hockey in England, as well as shinny, ricket, and ice polo in North America. Add in Native American lacrosse and shinny with some rugby-football and an ice-skating pastime and what happens is hockey. Like Canada itself, hockey is made up of a peculiar mosaic of northern European 'immigrant' and indigenous North American customs. That may be why it means so much to Canadians. Hockey is who we are.

Let's take each contributing sport in this landscape, dig down to the genealogical roots, and see how they collectively blossomed into the world's fastest sport. Then, maybe, we will know "How Hockey Happened."

The origin of Canada's ice game has been debated almost since the first puck was shot. This artist illustrated the topic by adapting a roller polo sketch to ice.

"There were several variations of the basic (shinny) game, including one played on ice."
— Joseph B. Oxendine
American Indian Sports Heritage, 1988

CHAPTER I
Gughawat (Indian shinny)
A very old game . . .

"What do you mean by 'hockey?'" That's the question I pose when people ask me, "Where was the game born?" Is true hockey the jazzed up professional game seen on television – or that lively amateur game played at the local arena — or the free-wheeling, outdoor shinny games of our youth?

If hockey is the true Canadian game, shouldn't its genesis be traceable to its native soil and soul? So, why not start this search with the first known occupants of North America and European immigrants' early contacts with them?

According to one Canadian historian, British troops, on arrival in Nova Scotia, saw natives playing a stick-ball game that they had adapted to play on the ice. While those Europeans brought with them memories of their own field games, it is not too much of a stretch of the imagination to be convinced that Woodland tribes of eastern North

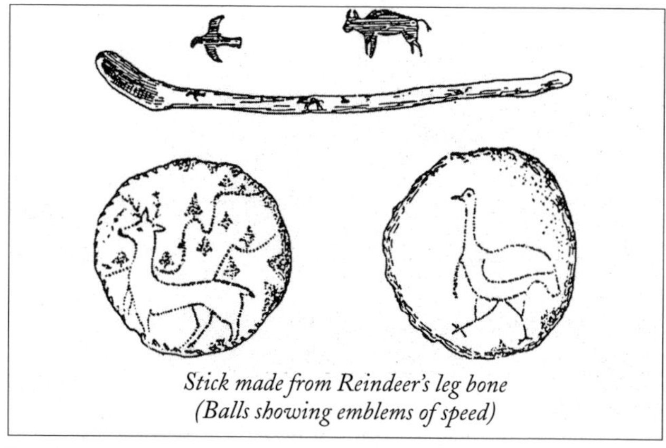
Stick made from Reindeer's leg bone (Balls showing emblems of speed)

American Indians at Hockey.

Lacrosse, or baggataway, was played throughout North America many years before there were international boundaries. The only boundary was the goal — usually two upright poles.

There was little difference between the native games of lacrosse and shinny. The action featured curved sticks and fierce battles for a ball.

America, inventors of the canoe, toboggan, and snowshoe, whose brothers created another curved stick game, lacrosse, also fashioned the first crude implements to propel a ball across land or ice.

Native historians note that Indian shinny was frequently referred to in myths and repeated in tribal lore. Unfortunately, the aboriginal heritage, like the 'white' man's early history, suffers from the lack of written records. The white man hasn't helped the situation by creating entertaining but fallacious newspaper stories, such as the concocted tale about the origin of the word 'hockey', which is supposedly translated from 'Ho-ghee', an Iroquoian expression allegedly meaning, "It hurts!"

The aboriginal word-of-mouth history maintains that natives played a shinny type game before the arrival of Europeans. The claim provokes a Scottish verdict, which is unproven, but one can't completely disregard the recollections of a distinguished Nova Scotian M'ikmaq elder. Joseph C. (Joe) Cope (1859-1951), in a letter preserved in the papers of noted author Thomas C. Raddall, passed on some enlightening information from his father, who died in 1913, aged 93. "Long before the pale faces strayed to this country," he said in a letter to *The Halifax Herald* in April 1943, "the Micmacs were playing two ball games, a field game and an ice game which were identical in every way." Each had two goals, which the natives called "forts" that were defended by the owners.

Joe Cope claimed that "skateless" hockey games were played by residents of the Ship Harbour Reserve "about 100 years ago" (1843). They later moved 53 kilometers south-west to Dartmouth, across the harbour from Halifax, and played the games on Maynard and Oak Hill lakes.

There is no doubt that shinny was a most important and popular game played by aboriginal males and females, separately, and sometimes against each other. A century ago it was common throughout North America — from New Mexico to British Columbia and from Florida to Canada's east coast. Fifty-nine shinny-playing tribes are listed in Stewart Culin's *Games of North American Indians,* published in Washington in 1907 and

Native women played shinny exclusively and occasionally with males. This team of nine Utes posed proudly at Whiterocks, Utah.

reprinted in 1992. No fewer than 30 pages were required to describe the games of various tribes and to illustrate the curved, decorated sticks and the ball made of buckskin, buffalo hair, mahogany block, or knot of wood.

Four North American tribes played on fields ranging from 200 to 1,400 yards long, with goals marked by stakes or blankets. Among the Pacific northwest Makah, said Culin, shinny was played after the capture of a whale, with players chasing a ball made from the soft bone of that mammal.

A pre-game feature of Indian shinny, sometimes referred to as "gughawhat," was wagering, a custom adopted later by white spectators, but barred to Native participants. "First one warrior advanced and threw down a robe before the old men [appointed to act as umpires]," reported George P. Belden, an observer of a Dakota shinny game. "Then a warrior from the other side came forward and laid a robe upon, so all bet, one against the other." The betting pot contained native products such as moccasins, ear rings, necklaces, bows and arrows and even ponies. The white man's influence was evident by others who bet hunting knives, gun powder, and hand mirrors. All were matched with appropriate items.

The game was started "by placing the ball in a hole in the centre of the field," noted Joseph B. Oxendine, author of *American Indian Sports Heritage*. Another option called for a neutral person to throw the ball high into the air, as is done in Celtic stick-ball games of hurling and shinty.

"When the players are well chosen — 10 to 100 aside and stripped naked except for loin cloths and moccasins ... it is often an interesting game," wrote Culin, a nineteenth-century ethnologist. "But when one of them, either intentionally or by accident, hurts another by a stroke with the play stick, a general shindy takes place and sticks are employed over each other's heads." Shindy is described as "a row, or a rumpus" as in "shin-dig," a common occurrence in Scottish shinty and today's ice hockey.

A modern dissenting opinion was voiced by Mohawk historian Jacob E. Thomas of the Sixth Nations, who lectures at Trent University in Peterborough, Ontario. "The Iroquois would not deliberately injure a man in the game, he said in 1981, as it would be "a sin to do so." Chief Jacob, interviewed for the McMichael Canadian Collection exhibit, *Soultenders and Goaltenders* (Native and Hockey Masks), said the Iroquois used a stuffed, moose-hair ball for a puck. Their hockey-shinny game was played on ice or "crusty snow" to a score of "three or seven or a multiple of seven," as frequently determined by a medicine man.

In Culin's day, the wooden implement was described as three-and-a-half feet long and "turned up at the lower end." The players, many of them "with their bodies painted in every possible variety of manner," some designated as defenders

The Mi'kmaqs of Nova Scotia made some of the first hockey sticks and sold them across North America under the "MicMac" or "Rex" brand names. The craft of making one-piece sticks was carried on in King's County into the 1920s.

and others as attackers, attempted to knock the ball through a goal marked by two posts. Many Indians could propel the ball 200 to 300 yards across the prairie. The team that scored two out of three times was judged the conqueror.

Did the aboriginal field game branch into ice hockey, as reported by Nova Scotian author Thomas Raddall in *Halifax — Warden of the North*? Not according to Dr. Oxendine, a one-time chancellor of the University of North Carolina. "Although several authors observed shinny being played on snow or ice, they never mentioned the use of ice skates and there was no indication that the ball was hit along the ice instead of in the air." Nevertheless, Oxendine feels that the descriptions of play suggest that shinny was a forerunner to both ice hockey and the game of field hockey.

In Nova Scotia, the involvement of the Mi'kmaq in the early development of stick-ball games is evident. Timothy (Ted) Graham, who grew up in Dartmouth lakes district, where many of the nineteenth-century games were played, put his thoughts of the 1870s on record in a 1943 letter: "We played with the Indians, who would play in moccasins, or wood skates. They could run like moose on the ice and were very rough in their style of play."

A decade earlier, when the birthplace of hockey debate was starting to simmer across Canada, the Canadian Press carried a report out of Sault Ste. Marie, Ontario, which indicates that other first nation members were experimenting with a stick-ball game on ice. The year was 1870, and the place was Bruce Mines in the Algoma district. Three young Indians on skates, "carrying long, pipe-shaped sticks," vied for possession of a small object, the story goes. "Soon a number of young men and boys procured sticks from the shore and joined in the play. Within a few days, a dozen or so of young white boys, with sticks similar to those used by the Indians joined 'Bobowash' (Louis Jack) Michigan Tomcat... and other Indians who had already developed into experts at the new game." Play covered six miles of smooth-as-glass ice, out the north channel gap of Georgian Bay to Hilton Wharf. Oldtimers claimed it to be the first of real ice hockey games — two cultures joining in healthy recreation without a sign of violence.

While Dr. Oxendine maintained that a high standard of sportsmanship was a common characteristic of Indian sports activity, there is evidence that fisticuffs did break out, as happens today in Canadian ice hockey. Some aboriginals had an answer for such outbreaks. Referees or judges, all highly respected elders, watched the lacrosse action, and whenever players lost their tempers and started to fight, they would be beaten with sticks "until the skirmishes ceased." This is not the answer to fighting in the professional game today, but the tradition of violence in the ice sports runs deep.

In 1966, the dean of Canadian sports writer, H.H. Roxborough, delved into the roots of lacrosse and hockey in his seminal book, One Hundred – Not Out.

“Hurley or hurling, an Irish variation of hockey may be the oldest form of a hockey-like game.”
—Wayne Simpson, *A Concise History of Sport in Canada*, 1989

CHAPTER 2

Hurling

A rough and rude game . . .

While hockey certainly took on some of the character of the Native American games of gugahawat and shinny, we need go abroad to seek out a variety of other games that help unravel hockey’s rich and rousing beginnings.

Ireland’s national game of hurling, described as the most ancient of stick-ball games, has been cited and celebrated, but not proven by Nova Scotian sources as the precursor of the Maritime version of what became Canadian hockey.

Hurling or caman — to address it by its Gaelic name — is almost as old as Ireland itself. As an ordinary pastime or inter-parish contest in the seventeenth century, the country’s national game was described by Christina Hole in *English Sports and Pastimes* (1949) as “a rude and rough game” played over hills and dales and sometimes on beaches. The players, as many as 50 aside, wielded short, broad-bladed sticks or hurleys (camans) and pursued a hard, round ball (sliotar). In 1698, an English traveller, John Dunton, gave one of the first descriptions of the pastime. “Goals were 200 to 300 yards apart, on a level plain, the barer of grass the better.” In County Kerry and other parts of southern Ireland, the game was immensely popular, and the rules were simple. In one version of the pastime, there was no such restriction as offside. It was a free-flowing melee.

In fact, in the late nineteenth century, there were two versions of the game. Paul Healy in his 1998 book, *Gaelic Games*, said the Dublin style of “hurley” was a much softer and less physical game than “hurling” and more similar to field hockey. “Hurley was effectively ignored, ground-hurling was incorporated into the more exciting aerial hurling, or else allowed to peter out.” Seamus J. King, author of *A History of Hurling*, confirms this viewpoint. “The evolution in the shape of the hur-

Ireland's national game of hurling was played by barefoot boys, according to this 1841 engraving. Their sticks, made of ash, were almost identical to early ice hockey sticks.

ley [stick] came with the change in the game from the late [eighteen] sixties, from the slower game that emphasized ground hurling, hip-to-hip combat, and encounters of strength."

There were two forms of traditional hurling in the 1850s, said King. "Commons" was played in the winter "on a restricted field of play" and resembled field hockey or the Scottish game of shinty. Players used a thin, crooked stick to propel a hard ball. The other version, "baile," was a summer game that needed a large area and was played mainly in southern Ireland. Players used a broad "caman" and a softer ball that could be lifted by the hand to be struck, and play was more violent.

Samuel Carter Hall, in his book *Ireland* (1857), explained how a match was commenced by choosing one person to throw up the ball between the unclad gladiators with their hurleys held high and prepared to strike it on its descent. "Now comes the crash of mimic war, hurleys rattle against hurleys — the ball is struck and restruck, often for several minutes, without advancing much nearer to either goal." And then Hall outlined a custom that distinguishes hurley from field hockey. "The tact and skill in taking it (the ball) on the point of the hurley, and running with it half the length of the field, and when too closely pressed, striking it (in mid-air) towards the goal, is a matter of astonishment to those who are but slightly acquainted with the play. ... It is often attended with dangerous, and sometimes with fatal results."

To be an expert hurler, *Chambers's Information for People* stated in 1857, a man must have a quick eye, a ready hand, a strong arm, and "be a good runner and a skilful wrestler." When two men grappled in this "fine, manly exercise," one fall only was allowed, while the rest of the players pursued the ball. As John Dunton explained the combative spirit: "Sometimes if he [a player] miss his blow at the ball, he knocks one of the opposers down; at which no resentment is to be shown. They seldom

The Irish game of hurling has made few inroads in Canada, but the Gaelic Athletic Association found Irish football more popular.

An old-style "hurl" (stick) is displayed by a young hurler in boots. In some areas of Ireland, hurling was more of a ground game and known as "hurley."

come off without broken heads or shins, in which they glory very much."

The Earl of Suffolk elaborated on another aspect of special hurling skills in 1896. "Taking the ball into the hand by means of the hurley, by catching it when it is in the air or on the hop is a good smart play. ... Raising the ball with the 'boss' or blade of the hurley and striking it in mid-air is a graceful and telling stroke." This essentially constituted what was called "aerial hurling."

Attacking players who broke in on the goalkeepers and those awarded a penalty shot were said to have been given a clear or free "puck," which means a "free shot." The Irish game would donate this name later to the distinctive object of pursuit in Canada's ice game.

Hurling, despite its long history, was slow to develop into an organized or systemized sport. It was not until 1879, long after the first field hockey rules were written, that the modern rules of hurling were drawn up at Trinity College, Dublin "to foster the noble and manly game of hurley in this its native country." These inaugural regulations were reportedly drawn up by the university hurley club for a city league that made contact with field hockey clubs in England. This six-club hurley union, said Ulster's Neil Garnham in *The Oxford Companion to Irish History*, was seen "as elitist and pro-Union" and was dissolved a few years after the Gaelic Athletic Association was formed in 1884 to govern hurling. Ironically, Dublin's first code, which was written about the time that the first regulations were being formulated for Canadian ice hockey, had a short life span.

Twenty-one players constituted a team when the Gaelic Athletic Association (G.A.A.) defined the rules in 1884. Years later, the number of players was reduced to 17, and still later, to 15 — which is the required number today.

In the meantime, emigrating Irishmen had taken the game to North America, where it reigned briefly, sputtered, and almost died. Historian Seamus J. King said Americans' perception of the game as "a dangerous sport" heightened its demise, though the American game is still played sporadically from coast to coast. The field variety of the game spread to San Francisco, California in 1863, to New York City in 1867, and to Boston, Massachusetts 12 years later. In that period before the G.A.A. was formed in 1884, according to writer Patrick F. McDevitt, games resembled nothing more than a faction fight, "with large, uneven groups of men hacking and wrestling as often as they followed the ball."

Early hurling had a rocky road in Canada. Hardy Irish immigrants, hired to do the backbreaking work in digging canals in Quebec (Montreal/Lachine), Nova Scotia (Shubenacadie), and Kingston, Ontario (Rideau), worked off any excess energy playing hurley in 1828. By 1862, members of Toronto's Irish community were playing hurling, along with Irish football at Queen's

Twentieth century players with broad-bladed sticks await a throw-in from the legendary Michael Collins at Dublin's crowded Croke Park stadium. Hurling matches were described as "Ireland's Olympic Games."

The ball-bat elements of Irish hurling are captured in logo form by Graham Thew Design for Seamus J. King's definitive History of Hurling, *published in 1998.*

Park. According to Dennis Ryan and Kevin Wamsley, writing in the *Canadian Journal of Irish Studies* (Spring 2004), "hurling was a Gaelic spectacle of some popularity" in the Ontario capital. Members of the Hibernian Benevolent Society competed for a handsome cup, which was displayed later at the home of the man who had scored "two of the three games" or goals. This "national separatist" organization even took the game on excursions to Buffalo, New York.

Rules were few for the Irish hurlers who settled in Nova Scotia. They accepted any number of players whenever their labours permitted it. A game between schoolboys on the ice of Long Pond near King's College in Windsor was referred to by Sam Slick's author Thomas Haliburton in an 1844 book of fiction as "hurley on the ice" without any mention of numbers — or skates. That activity was alleged to have occurred in the first decade of the nineteenth century, when strapped-on-skates were more conducive to pleasure skating than to the stops, starts, and sudden turns of a rousing match of hurling.

Hurling or hurley was played summer and winter, on foot or skates or both, by Irishmen working on the Shubenacadie Canal near Dartmouth, Nova Scotia in the 1820s, by women skaters on Lily Lake at Saint John, New Brunswick in 1833, and by Mount Allison University students at Sackville, New Brunswick in the 1840s.

Players pursued a heavy leather-covered ball, described by an "old boy" in *The Argosy* as "a very ugly missile about one's shins." A Pictou, Nova Scotia editor, Jonathan Blanchard, a native of New Hampshire, confirmed this thought in 1829 when he reported the first case of a stick-ball action with players wearing something other than the usual

In the United States, the game was portrayed by illustrators as violent and dangerous, where ambulance attendants were on call to care for the wounded.

boots: “Every idler ... may turn out with skates on feet, hurly in hand and play the delectable game of break-shins.” The camans (home-hewn sticks) were also dangerous to other extremities, which appears to indicate Maritimers were following the Irish aerial game rather than the field or ground hockey. A champion Mount Allison University player in the 1840s “with arms like a son of Arak,” said a theologian, could propel the ball “like a cannon ball and clear a clean lane through the players.”

The hurleys hit more than a ball in those swash-buckling school-day struggles. Another “Mount A” student, Andrew Purdy, in a letter to his father in 1846, explained how he was clipped over the left eye from the wayward stick of an opponent in a yard game. “Although it is not cut it is pretty badly bruised,” he wrote. “The cause of its not being cut is on account of the shape of the stick, it being quite round and smooth.” In another incident, John Cunard, who studied at King’s College (1816-1818), had his front teeth knocked out with a hurley by Pete Delaney of Annapolis Valley.

Despite its hazards, the Irish game survived in another form and under other names. In fact, names given to these recreational games on ice depended on the birthplace or experience of the viewer of the action. A Scots’ observer would immediately label any stick-ball game as “shinty.” An English man would say the game is “bandy” or “hockey on the ice.” Native Canadians and later generation Canadians would refer to it as “shinny.” But in the Maritimes, with its influx of British troops and its mix of immigrants, the locals championed “hurly’ and would create new names for the simple contest of trying to put an object through a goal.

Today, crowds of up to 75,000 fill Dublin’s Croke Park to see men from Munster and Leinster, wearing helmets and colourful shirts marred by advertising logos, compete in the All-Ireland finals. Men who play for the sheer joy of the game clash in action described as “fast, exciting, barbaric and regulated mayhem,” while female teams meet in a somewhat restrained version of the game called “camogie.”

In New York City, the centre of the American game, sons of Eire have crowded the Polo Grounds and Celtic Park for exhibitions of “the world’s greatest stick game” by touring teams from Ireland. Each September in Bedford, near Halifax, where ground hurling was once played for Queen Victoria’s Jubilee, as many as 60 expatriates gather with their Guinness in O’Toole’s Roadhouse to soak up the live television action and nostalgic reminiscences.

John Toole, an itinerant Irish portrait painter, captured the crash and smash of a stick-ball game in this scene from Virginia in the 1840s.

Ho for shinties flashing / On some chosen lea! /
Of all games surpassing / That's the game for me.
—Evan MacColl, *Poems and Songs*, 1883

CHAPTER 3
Shinty
That's the game for me!

As ancient as is the Irish game of hurling, the national Scottish game of shinty — with similar Gaelic roots – is an antiquated one and probably the father or grandfather of Canadian shinny. Its origin is as almost obscure as its name, which since the late 1700s has been variously recorded as shiney, shinney, and shinnie. Each has been used to describe the game, the ball (of wood, hair, or bone), or the stick.

The game's objective, as noted by an observer in the early 1800s, was simple: "The performers were divided into two sections and were armed with long sticks called shinties. A ball was thrown between the contending forces and hit and driven hither and thither, until finally it was driven beyond the bourne [limit or goal] on either side and whoever reached the goal claimed the victory."

The participants were usually the hardy highlanders of northern Scotland. It was their custom to play shinty in the winter season when large parties assembled during the Christmas season. By 1836 Londoners were entertained by Gaelic songs of exiled Scots "in praise of the shinnie."

"This game is often played upon the ice by one parish against another," noted Sir Eneas Mackintosh in describing the every-day life of an old highland farm. The prize was a cask of whisky. Shinty (camac) was honoured in song and "dignified in the heroic verse of *The Grampians Desolate*," as recorded by Robert Scott Fittis in *Sports and Pastimes of Scotland* (1891):

The appointed day is come — the eventful day
When on the snowy field, in firm array,
Glen meeting glen — yet no with tempered blades,
But sapling-oaks cut from the neighbouring glades
Engage with ardour keen — in jovial guise,
A cask of whisky strong, the victory's prize!

Scottish highlanders created the ancient game of shinty — a wild, stick-ball contest that Irishmen claim is an offspring of hurling.

Cartoonists have fun depicting the violent aerial collisions. Shinty is started by throwing a ball up between two centres.

Lead to the contest fierce their marshalled ranks;
To wield their weapons — namely, shinny shanks.
Behold the victor, with joy-beaming eyes,
Triumphant marches with the well-won prize,
And in the hall aloft 'tis placed with care,
That all anon may drink a liberal share.

Emigrating sons of Scotland took the game and its custom to Canada. One of the first references to shinty in North America was recorded in Kingston, Upper Canada, in 1839. The convivial Scots, who formed a third of the town's population, met at an expatriate's store to plan the game on one of their favourite days, New Year's. "About 300 persons, including spectators assembled on the ice in front of the town," reported *The Kingston Chronicle and Gazette* after the 1840 match. "The ball was flung up in the air between the two adverse chieftains as the signal to commence hostilities and immediately a most vigorous contest was begun and maintained nearly three hours with unabated energy." The newspaper was pleased to report that there was no accident or quarrelling for the second exhibition of "the manly and noble game."

The custom of "the vigorous and cohesive Scots community of Kingston" for an annual game continued until at least 1843 when the natives of Argyle and Ross-shire, 28 to a side, met on the parade ground of Point Frederick, now the site of the Royal Military College of Canada. "After a severe contest of three hours," the newspapers reported, "each party gained one hail [goal] and night coming on denied them the opportunity of playing a third. ... To show that everything passed off with the greatest good feeling, the participants marched home with their clubs over their shoulders and a pair of bagpipers playing before them, with flags flying and after taking a glass of `mountain dew' they parted, looking forward to another meeting."

Kingston was capital of the United Provinces of Canada at that time, and one of the observers of winter pastimes was a young lawyer and future prime minister, John Alexander Macdonald, who was five years old when his parents emigrated from Glasgow in 1820. There is no evidence that

Kilts swung and banners waved when Scotsmen clashed in annual shinty games in the Highlands.

the future prime minister, then a budding alderman in the town of Kingston, took in the annual shinty matches, but he did award cash prizes for speed-skating races on Kingston harbour ice.

The Sons of Scotland played the game wherever they settled. In Montreal, their enthusiasm for the exercise was such that the city council banned the game along with skating and sledding on city streets. In Bytown, the lumbering settlement that would be re-named Ottawa, shinney, "minus ice and skates," was played on Wellington Street in the 1840s. The Scotsmen of New Edinburgh played "shintie" against plain-clothed men of town on the Ottawa River ice on Christmas Day, 1852. The victors "in Scottish costume" (kilts) were so proud of their victory that they struck an engraved silver medal to commemorate the event. Once displayed in Ottawa's Bytown Museum, the medal bore the names of the Gaelic Burghers: Lumsden, Grant, Cameron, Fraser, McDonald and the Masson brothers, Hugh and Donald.

In the United States, "old fashioned games, practised from time immemorial," were played in New England. Two dozen "shinties" were imported for the New York Caledonian games in 1856.

Back in the land of the heather in the middle of the nineteenth century, shinty declined in popularity and lived only in the Scottish glens of Lochaber, Strathglass, and Badenoch. Decades

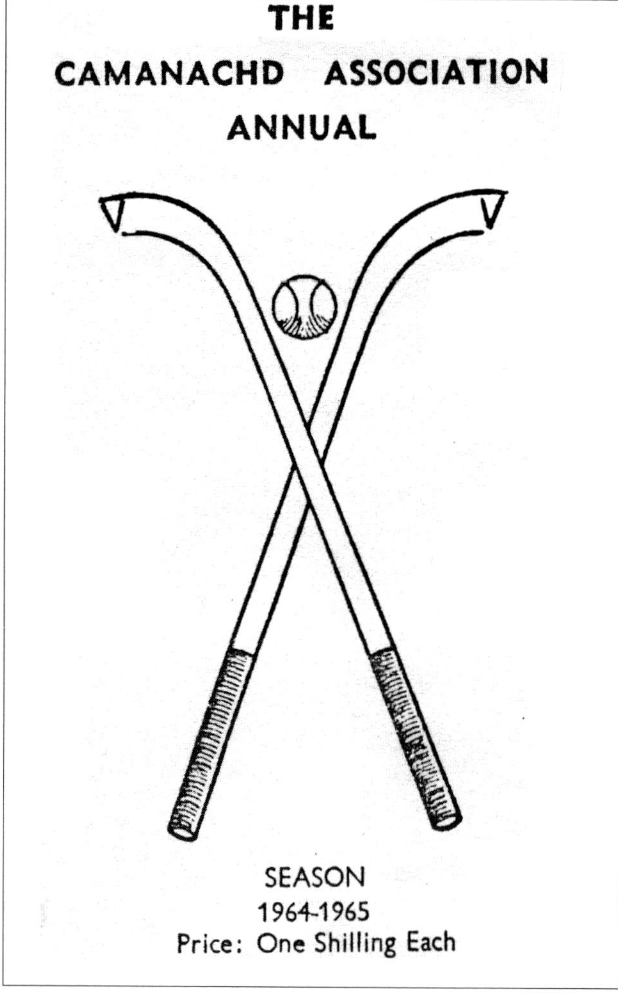

The Commanachd Association established the modern rules of shinty long after ice hockey rules were formulated. The blades of the sticks had a triangular shape to facilitate chipping or long drives, as in golf.

Kingston artist Jillian Hulme Gilliland captures the one-on-one duel of two kilted shinty players.

The early sticks had club-like heads for long hits down field.

later, long after other stick-ball games had been codified, a Glassburn captain led the revival of the pastime by publishing a code of rules that introduced the first 15-men teams at Inverness in 1873.

Shinty, yesterday and today, has a unique opening play, almost identical to the way a hurling match is commenced. "A ball was thrown [up] between the contending forces," wrote a Scotsman in the early 1800s. "It was hit and driven hither and thither, until finally it was driven beyond the bourne [boundary] on either side and whoever reached the goal claimed victory." A century and a half later, Scotland's highland game is played in a confined space with the same energy, precision, passionate fury. Said UK-born Peter Alliss, a noted ABC-TV golf commentator about the modern players: "They play like demented demons!"

In Canada, as the Scots' community integrated into Canadian pastimes, "shinty" disappeared, but "shinny" became a part of every boy's language, and this pastime — whether enjoyed on ice, asphalt, or grass — remains popular to this day.

Meanwhile in Northern California, Scottish expatriates and American colleagues have revived shinty. They play with six or 12 players on a soccer-size pitch and demonstrate the game at Highland games. Perhaps Canadian sports buffs will get an opportunity to see shinty re-introduced to Scots' gatherings at Highland games in such keen Scottish communities as Fergus and Maxville in Ontario.

When North Americans transferred stick-ball games to ice, the result was not always rousing action, as the tranquility of this engraved scene shows.

CHAPTER 4
Shinny

The crude and exciting game . . .

"Shinny was played on the lakes, rivers and canals throughout the country, but only a discerning eye could discover in this crude, but infatuating amusement, the grand possibilities that a refined game could offer."

— Arthur Farrell, *Hockey, Canada's Royal Winter Game*, 1899

"What is so rare as a day in June, if ever come perfect days?" Wordsworth once asked. With apologies to the great English poet, may I pose the question: What is so rare as a day in January, with a clear sheet of natural ice, and a horde of stick-carrying skaters chasing a round object?

Canadian youths today, who play shinny-hockey on indoor artificial ice arenas, are in their element there, but they know little of the joy of the original shinny game played on some wind-swept or sun-blessed slough or peaceful pond. CBC's Fred McInnis succinctly summed up the scene in 1996: "No time, no sides, no rules." As Marc Baril stated in his January 2005 "Frozen Pond" essay in *The Ottawa Citizen*, "Most youngsters will grow up in the local house and travel leagues, yet very few will ever experience the game the way it was meant to be played; beyond the confines of unforgiving boards and state-of-the-art Plexiglas, free from the ear-piercing laments of overzealous coaches and obsessed parents."

While Canadians may think that shinny — "hockey's pure, original form" — is an exclusive Canadian game, there is evidence that the ground game was played in a variety of forms in what became the United States of America. In some of the states, it was known by the name of 'hockey" and 'bandy,' stated Jennie Holliman of Columbia University in her 1931 thesis, reprinted by Porcupine Press in 1975 as *American Sports (1785-1835)*. "Shinny was a favourite college sport and was played until football became a recognized sport in the 'forties and baseball in the 'fifties. The sport was so violent and produced such physical injuries that it was discouraged … [and] was prohibited at Princeton in 1787."

An American college coach, Eddie Jeremiah, described shinny in 1942 as "disorganized play."

Any frozen pond where two or a dozen skaters gathered together was ideal for shinny. There was just one rule – "Shinny on your own side."

This artist's conception of a Tam-O-Shanter topped youth in Montreal represents Scots who moved shinty to the ice and called it "shinny."

Another American author, Al Hirschberg, dismissed it as "a higgledy-piggledy (helter-skelter) sort of game with no indeterminate rules and no particular pattern." A Canadian male, released to the unlimited bounds of open, outdoor ice, and no referee restrictions, might tag the activity as "Freedom Fifteen!" There is no greater joy for a boy on skates with a stick and a ball and a vast expanse of ice ahead and opponents in pursuit.

A few oldtimers can recall when shinny was played without goals. The main objective was rather to single-handedly "rag" the puck or frozen "horse bun" for as long as opponents would permit. Hall of Famer Bobby Orr, a stickhandling wizard, who retained possession of the puck or ball on the Seguin River near his Parry Sound, Ontario home, called the pastime "Keep Away." Today, modern shinny addicts refer to it as "hog" as in "puck hog."

No one described the original shinny more entertainingly than an English emigrant sportsman, J.J. Rowan, during his 1865 tour of Canada. Visiting a New Brunswick village in the Bathurst area, he spotted a diminutive French (Acadian) boy, an excellent skater, carrying a crooked stick, who met some boys playing what he called hockey. "Putting the crooked end of his stick to the ice and seizing it with both hands, he plunged into the thickest of the fray. In [seconds] he was out again at the other side, zig-zagging like a jack-snipe,

Canadians think of shinny as a Canadian created game, but American boys with stick and ball played the game in the mid-1800s, as this Nathaniel Currier engraving attests.

Scottish shinty sticks were narrow weapons, swung high and low in early melees.

shoving the ball before him and pursued by at least 20 youths. They could not touch him. He did just what he liked with the ball, three or four of them lay sprawling on the ice."

About the same time in the Montreal area, the game of shinny without goals was much enjoyed. The object of pursuit varied according to the occasion, W.L. (Chick) Murray told *The Gazette* of Montreal in 1936: "It was played by boys who would chase a small block of wood, a battered tin can or any similar object which could be batted along the ice. If no one liked the other's 'puck' a little better than their own, it was not unusual for some of them to dash in, steal the puck and skate away with it. The result was a melee!"

There were no goals and no rules in the first recorded account of pure shinny. As *The Acadian Recorder* of Halifax reported in 1895: "Shinney is played on the ice in the open air and the opposing teams are made up of two disorderly mobs of unlimited number of players, who use little system and have, but a single object in view ... the driving of the ball across the goal line or between the goals posts of the opposing team." Years later, as hockey became an organized game indoors, shinny was played on any available sheet of ice, sans rules and referee, but with chunks of ice, boots, jackets, or blocks of wood to mark the goal posts.

Montreal boys used to play "shinney," said 80-year-old Henry Joseph in 1943, "but they played it on the streets or ponds minus the use of skates." The modern Canadian version was definitely played on skates, which distinguished shinny from the original Scottish field game of shinty. To some expatriate Scotsmen, shinty/shinny could be

Players of all ages pause for a photographer on this low-boarded rink on Wolfe Island near Kingston, Ontario. Men, boys and the parish priest joined in the 1920s action.

played on any surface. A Perth, Ontario native, Ron MacFarlane, recalls the confusion when his grandfather asked his skate-toting grandson, "Are you going to play shinny on the ice?" The young Canadian, later a judge, asked under his breath: "Where else?"

Any number of males could participate in early shinny, as indicated by historian Edward S. Horsey, who saw Kingston, Ontario garrison soldiers play the sport as early as 1860: "They could cut the figure S and other fancy figures but shinney was their delight. Crowds would be placed at Victoria or Shoal Tower [a limestone redoubt near Kingston's new City Hall] and 50 or more players on each side would be in the game."

While the military members may have fashioned their sticks in field-hockey style, nineteenth century rural Canadians invented implements that were vastly different from the multi-coloured, lacquered and well-manicured composite sticks of today's hockey game. "The sticks ... were crude, home-made affairs, which were procured by pulling up a young maple sapling by the roots and using the curved main tap-root as the blade," reminisced Dr. Arthur G. Dorland, 78, a former Prince Edward County resident in *Former Days and Quaker Ways,* published by *The Picton Gazette* in 1965. "Some of the sticks were so clumsily and badly shaped that they were little more than clubs by which its wielder tried to bludgeon his way through the field towards the opposing goal." The game was a strenuous one, he said, unhampered by any particular rules. And the object of attack was anything from a ball to a block of wood, flat stone, or a frozen ball of "horse-dung."

Pratfalls were part of the game when shinny was played outdoors.

Stick-swinging shinny players are front and centre in this Toronto harbour winter scene captured in watercolour by William Armstrong in 1852.

In some versions of the Canadian game, there was one main law or understanding: "Each player must 'shinny on his own side' — that is, he must always play with his left side toward the goal that he is attacking, as right-handed players usually do," it was explained as late as 1956 in an educational book on games. Holliman said the "shinny on your own side" rule was in effect in early American games. Her description of the play was unique: "Opposing parties, according to rules, were not allowed to place themselves otherwise than face to face ... the temptation was to get upon the opposite side and strike with the enemy. But the cry of 'shinny on your own side' stopped such movement."

As in pick-up games today, the players reach a general understanding of any regulations or customs that might be followed. In the Depression days of the 1930s, I thought "shinny-on-your-own- side" meant play with one team only and did not indicate what side of the stick you could use to shoot or pass. The latter requirement is a holdover from the original rules of English field hockey that stipulated all players must shoot right-handed and had to reverse their sticks to pass backwards in the other direction. Canadian shinny provided the freedom of stickhandling and passing on the forehand or backhand.

The famous Brampton sportsman W. Perkins Bull had another version of the game, which he elucidated in *From Rattlesnake Hunt to Hockey*, published in 1934: "The only restriction appears to have been that the player must remain behind the puck, or be 'onside,' that he must `shinny on his own side.'" This fits into the early onside rule for organized hockey. Bull also pointed out that skates were not light metal tubes riveted to specially-contrived boots, "but rough, awkward iron blades attached to frames made of smoothed wood which were screwed to the heels of the wearer's shoes and strapped over the instep."

The game was not confined to the ice of Canadian lakes and rivers. Shinny was popular on ponds in the United States. Walter Prichard Eaton (1878-1942) gave this description of the pastime in the American-based *Outing* magazine in 1913: "The two captains, elected by the rough democracy of boyhood, chose up sides, usually the smallest boy on each side was put in goal." The selection process has a modern day version called "Sticks," in which players throw their sticks in a pile and one assigned person separates them into two piles, thereby creating opposing teams. In Eaton's American version, the result was the same with 20 boys on a side — "big fellers and little fellers."

"When the ball was put in play you heard the rush and roar of all their runners and the clashing of their sticks as each individual player tried to get the ball into his possession and nurse it, dodging and doubling toward the enemy's goal. We knew nothing of the science of passing in those days,"

Shinny by moonlight or spotlight attracted tuqued youngsters at the frozen infield at the fairgrounds in Kingston, Ontario.

A prairie slough was a grand spot for two youths to scrimmage under parental supervision in the early 1900s.

Women and men, including a doctor, joined in this face-off photo on a frozen slough near Viking, Alberta.

Eaton added. "It was each man for himself and great was the honour to him who could get the ball away from [the future aircraft pioneer] Frank Wright in open field, as that hero of the ice ducked and dodged and evaded pursuit, keeping the ball against his stick with uncanny skill or shooting it past you only to pick it up again while you breathlessly stopped up and turned in vain pursuit. There were no periods. We played till we were exhausted."

"There was only one rule for shinny and that was *go to it*, but 'shinny on your own side,'" wrote *The Toronto Telegram*'s venerable columnist J.P. Fitzgerald in the midst of the birthplace of hockey debate in 1943. "It was played generally at least throughout the province of Ontario and even had one big annual game in most centres. ...The number on each side was as many as cared to take part and the ice surface was convenient even up to a quarter of a mile." Perkins Bull confirmed that the annual game celebration was common throughout the Province of Ontario in the "post pioneer days" of the 1880s. Teams divided between "east" and "west" met on the Credit River "before the entire village."

Some shinny matches were not recognizable by onlookers. On the bay at Toronto, where annual holiday matches became popular, an artist attracted by a steamboat, sketched the first shinny scrimmage — eight skaters with curved sticks duelling for an object. "The ice was covered by one restless throng from morning 'til night,' wrote George Stanley in *Life in the Woods* (1864). "Games of different kinds played between large numbers were very exciting. Scotchmen, with their curling, others (schoolboys) with balls, battering them hither and thither."

Today, energetic lads and lassies, repeat that scene everywhere, albeit in somewhat smaller confines and with fewer players. And hockey coaches, when their players slip into loose play, evoke the "shinny" name. When new forward passing rules are introduced, hockey is tagged as a "wild scramble from start to finish."

Is outdoor shinny dying in this age of global warming and recreation confined to numerous artificial ice rinks? Some environmentalists believe so. The season is shorter and there are fewer cold days, Global Exchange's Mike Hudema, was quoted by Canadian Press in November, 2005. Tired of playing games "on slush," the Edmonton, Alberta native plans to stage a mock funeral for shinny-hockey at a Montreal climate change conference. However, in Toronto, which must hold the record for outdoor artificial ice surfaces at 49, shinny survives even in the balmy temperatures of the winter of 2006. One January night, Dave Bidini, the author of *The Best Game You Can Name*, recalled seeing three or four kids playing shinny in the dark after scaling the wire fence of a neighbourhood rink. "That's the spirit of shinny," he told *The Globe and Mail.* As Ralph Benmurgi

Hockey or shinny was a co-ed game a century ago. This Orphan Annie-like figure demonstrates an early slap shot as she races toward hazardous ice.

stated on the CBC in New Year's Day, 2002, "Shinny is sort of an elastic type of game. The freedom of the game provides the opportunity to express yourself."

Ideal weather conditions or not, many Canadian boys will continue to grab a stick on mild days and shinny on roads, alleys, and playgrounds, and "express themselves" like Jarome Iginla, Dany Heatley, or the local hockey hero.

Minneapolis boys display a variety of sticks used to propel a tin-can puck. The Twin Cities' paper stated: "Shinny consisted of no set time, periods or limits beyond the natural endurance of the competitors."

A lone skater with a curved stick (right, foreground) shares the St. Lawrence River ice with other blade artists and iceboat sailors at Quebec in 1857.

> "They play hockey in England with round sticks and a ball and call it bandy."
> —*The Daily British Whig,* Kingston, 1902.

CHAPTER 5
Bandy
A rough and ready frolic

The on-ice game of bandy, still popular today in Scandinavia and Russia, has been cited as an obvious ancestor of ice hockey. The stick-ball pastime originated in England, and another form of the field game was played in Wales. "It is highly probable that this very ancient team game was the precursor of both field hockey and ice hockey and probably should be considered to be the inspiration for bandy," wrote Mark Heller in *Ice Skating,* published in 1979.

Like most stick-ball games, bandy started as a field or street game and was played on any suitable surface. Bandy has for ages been popular among the remnants of ancient Britons, who inhabit the vale of Glamorgan, reported *The Cricketer's Manual* in 1851. "The players in this locality are remarkably jealous respecting their bandy accomplishments, for they have long defied competition and the game stands at the top of the diversion list."

A top-hatted, English aristocrat (referee?) confronts a bandy player in regular sporting attire in this 1890s Charles Whymper engraving.

FEBRUARY 27, 1892.] PUNCH, OR THE LONDON CHARIVARI. 101

A MEETING OF THE "BANDY" ASSOCIATION

FOR THE PROMOTION OF "HOCKEY ON THE ICE."

A Punch *magazine artist pokes fun at these bow-legged, bandy players in 1892. Note the odd blocks of stone or ice that serve as goal posts.*

Bandy-ball, one of the ancient stick games, can be traced back to the 14th century.

The "rules" were simple and the similarity to field hockey was apparent: "A spot is selected on a hard field; two sets of players are arranged with bent or clubbed sticks, a ball is then set going and each party strikes it along to a certain mark or goal."

The name bandy has roots in the late seventeenth century, when a Yorkshireman was noted by English dramatist Thomas D'Urfey as being "the prettiest fellow at bandy," who obviously was not "bandy-legged" or "bow-legged." The anonymous Yorkshire gentleman in question was also good at the ancient and noble English game of cricket. The two old games have a language relationship. as noted by Robert Forby in his 1830 book on East Anglia vocabulary: "Of the several games at ball played with a bandy, that, in which a ball is aimed by one player at a wicket [goal], defended by the adversary with his bandy, must be allowed to be very appropriately called bandy-wicket." Years later, a Nova Scotian ice game would be called "wicket" or "ricket." On the Isle of Man in the Irish Sea between Ireland and Scotland, a probable stepping-stone in the spread of hurling to the land of the heather, bandy brought other problems. "We requested the police to put a stop to the dangerous game called bandy which the boys are playing on the quay, the pier and in various parts of the town," the *Manx Sun* reported in 1835. "Several gentlemen have had severe raps on the legs and no person is free from danger."

In England, the only stick-ball competition was field hockey, but the switch from ground to ice apparently occurred in the Fen district north of Cambridge. The low-lying land of Cambridgeshire and Lincolnshire, where centuries ago Romans and the Dutch created canals to drain the bog-like soil, records the first reference to the game on skates at the turn of the 18th century. It was a natural progression for Fenmen, most of

Two bandy players demonstrate "dribbling" or stickhandling on Fen skates in England in the 1890s.

whom where at ease on homemade blades and set early records for speed skating.

"Probably bandy was played on the ice before skates were in use, for the level and slippery ice would suggest a surface upon which a 'cat' (ball) could be easily and accurately driven," wrote C.G. Tebbutt, the father of English bandy, in *Skating*, the 1902 edition of *The Badminton Library*.

"But, when once the player was shod with skates, and could career over the ice at a great pace, could suddenly stop, and as suddenly start, could turn and dodge at full speed and maintain a pace impossible on land, then enthusiasm for bandy was assured; it became, in fact, to its devotees the most fascinating of games."

Some players used an inverted walking stick, but the majority played with hand-cut, homemade bandies. "For toughness, lightness and shape, the bandy is made of the bough of a pollard willow tree, … pollard ash or ground ash, which more often grows in the desired curve," Neville and Albert Goodman wrote in *Fen Skating* (circa 1882). "Bandies have not been sold in shops, but are either cut by the player, or are ordered of a village carpenter." These pioneer players gave an early description of stickhandling: "A stick … in the hand of a skilful player … is used for carrying on the ball by shoving and guiding, and only occasionally is it used for hard knocking."

A full-length bandy weighed about one pound

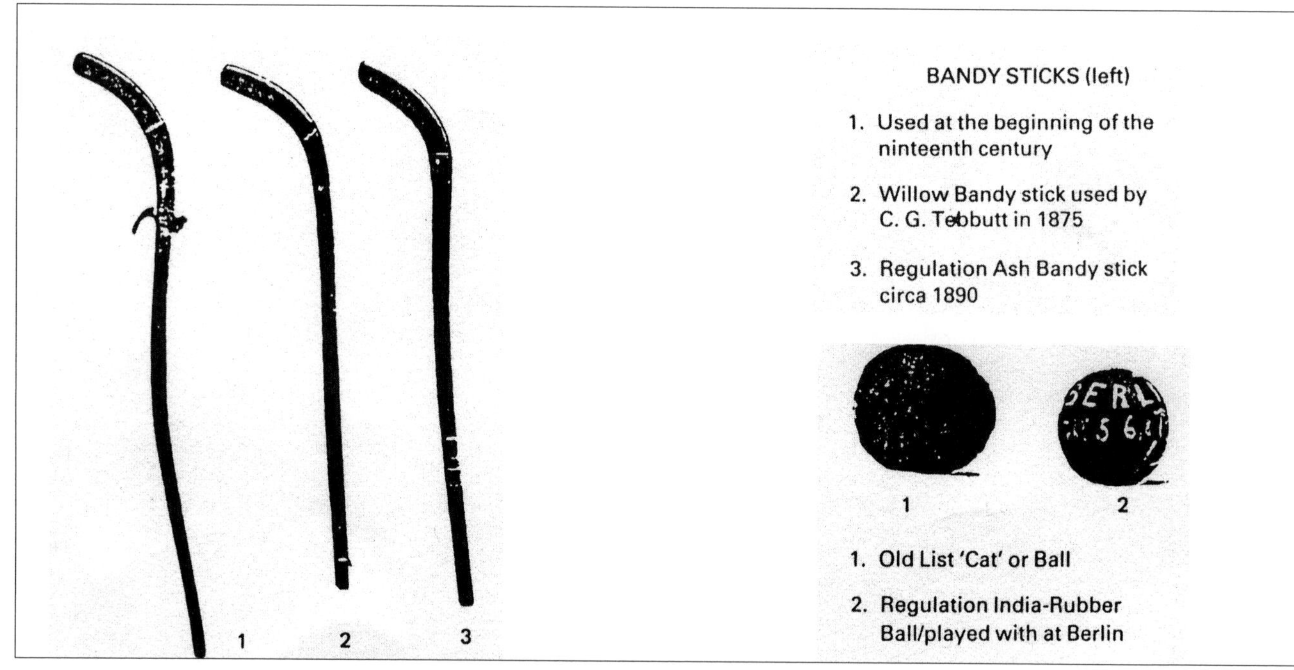

BANDY STICKS (left)

1. Used at the beginning of the ninteenth century
2. Willow Bandy stick used by C. G. Tebbutt in 1875
3. Regulation Ash Bandy stick circa 1890

1. Old List 'Cat' or Ball
2. Regulation India-Rubber Ball/played with at Berlin

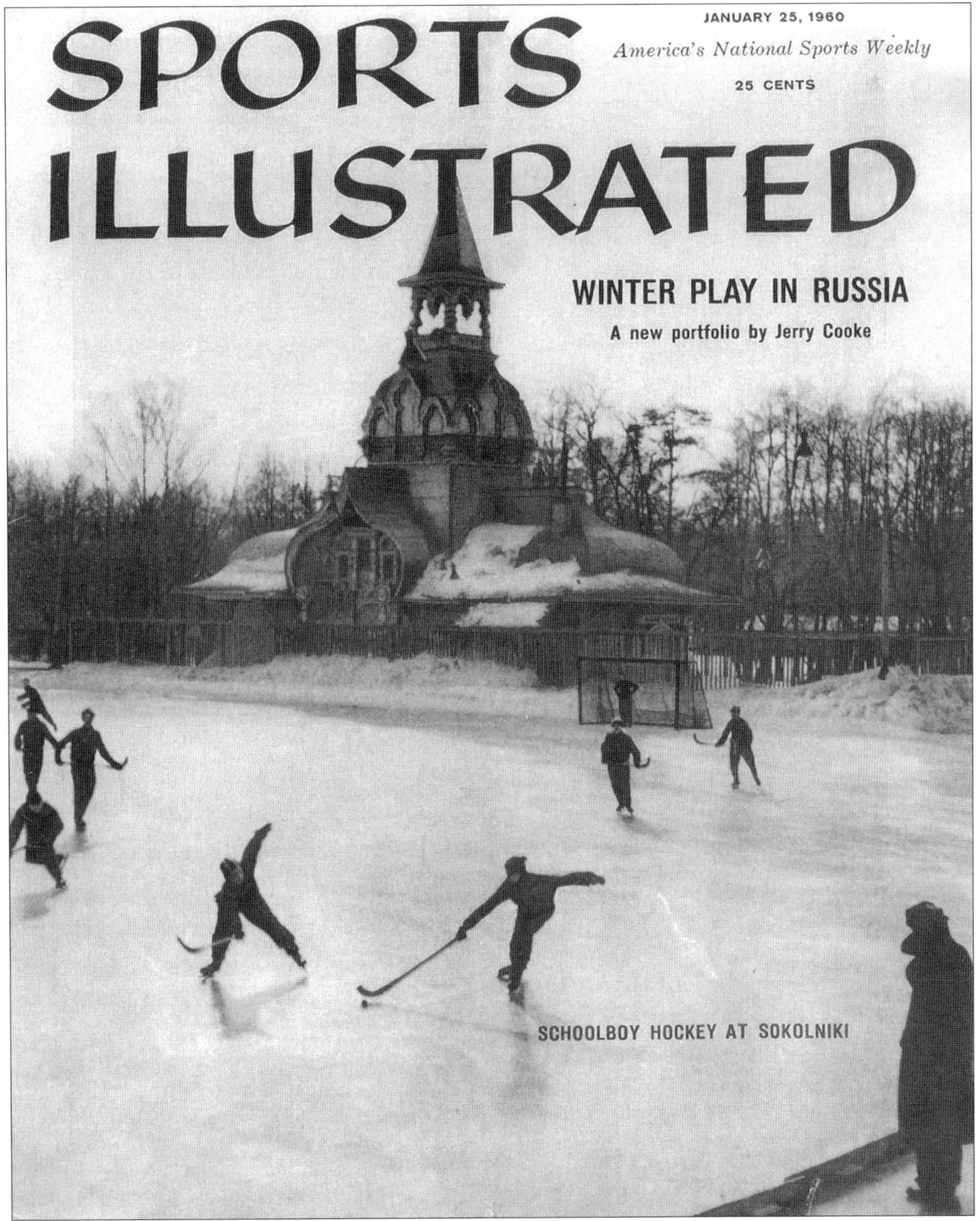

Sports Illustrated *revealed bandy to the world with this 1960 cover shot, but called it "hockey." Bandy players made the transition to hockey, and Soviet teams became world champions. Note the huge goal nets.*

This caricature of a cigar-smoking gentleman indicates bandy was first played on land.

and measured 39 inches (compared to today's hockey stick of 53 inches), but some Fenmen cut off three inches at each end so as to continually change it from hand to hand. All bandies were flat on both sides of the blade, while field hockey sticks were flat on the left side and rounded on the other. They could be used "to hit, catch, lift up or bear down the bandy of another opponent," but not swung with the intention of hitting, intimidating, catching, or tripping an opponent.

The site of early action among teams from towns along the River Ouse was confined only to the expanse of ice. The ball, originally made of cloth cuttings from the village tailor, was propelled by homemade sticks. "Few rules trammelled the freedom of the play and fewer disputes spoilt the enjoyment — a contract, alas, to some of the professional and even quasi-amateur games one now sees," said Ake Duner in reviewing 40 years of international bandy for a Swedish journal in 1995.

Challenge matches were the order of the day as the Bury Fen men north of Cambridge remained undefeated for a decade. By 1865, the game reached Nottingham and then travelled south to Virginia Water near Windsor Castle. By 1868 the Bury Fen team provided a double-header exhibition of the game on the ice at London's Crystal Palace. This friendly competition speeded the advent of a code of rules, and the first draft of regulations came at a meeting St. Ives in 1882. The rules resembled Association Football (soccer) with

A team of bandy players from Bury Fen, north of Cambridge, England, where bandy was born, pose with supporters in the 1890s.

The rules of bandy, formulated much later than Canadian ice hockey, are detailed and specific. They permit open ice skating and intricate passing plays on rinks the size of a soccer field.

a pitch 150 yards in length and 100 yards in wide, sticks no wider than two inches and no offside for players within the team's defending half of the ice.

By 1891, the Bandy Association in England was formed and rules framed that limited the players to 15 aside and set the goal size at 12 by 7 feet, compared to 6 feet wide in the early game. By the time the English had codified bandy, Canadians had already developed the early rules of ice hockey and organized league games and trophy competitions.

A Russian artist turned the kolfer, portrayed earlier (page 4), into a rushing bandy player for Anatoli Tarasov's 1972 book on hockey.

Bandy expanded to Holland, where an early form of the game was played, and then moved on to Sweden, Norway, Switzerland, and Russia. When World War I (1914-1918) and World War II (1939-1945) were fought, Canadians and their Russian allies contested for hockey supremacy. The two games of bandy and hockey met, and young Canucks, accustomed to ice hockey in confined indoor rinks, were extended to compete in the free skating game of bandy on football-sized fields. It was a sign of things to come in the international hockey world.

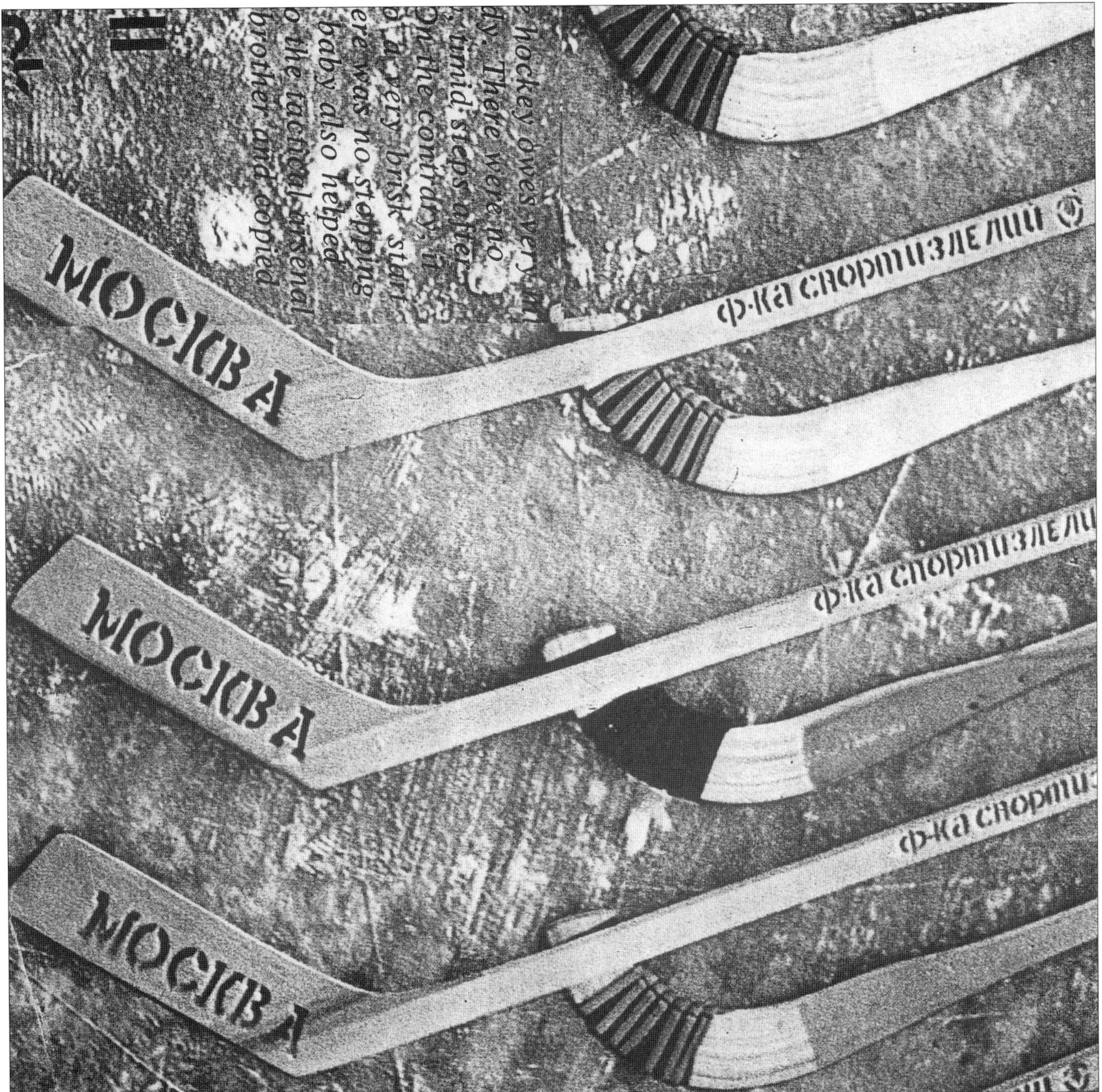

Modern bandy sticks — curved and bound — contrast with straight-cut Russian hockey sticks.

"Bell-ringing and playing at hockey are the worst vices of the depraved tinker."

—Lord Macaulay,
English historian (1800–1859)

CHAPTER 6
Field Hockey
Dangerous but elegant ...

The roots of today's hockey go deep into ancient civilizations — into Rome and possibly Persia. Stick-ball games are recorded in ancient Greek friezes and gloriously painted in early Flemish art. The modern cradle of the outdoor game, however, was England.

The game was not always well received. According to Britain's premier historian of the game, Nevil Miroy, field hockey was prohibited in 1363 and punishment for offenders was harsh. "Each player could be fined ten pounds and given two years in prison."

"It was played indiscriminately on the frozen ground or the ice in winter," the *Encyclopedia Britannica* summed up in 1911. "Play was crude, rough ... dangerous and rules were few," stated Norman Barrett in *Lonsdale Library's* 1955 version of the game in the 1800s.

Played casually by boys for a long time, it became "a man's game," Miroy notes. At Eton, it was played "with a considerable degree of dexterity," and he rated it as "one of the most elegant and gentlemanlike exercises." *The Book of Games* created one of the first dialogues in noting that a group of boys "with sort of hockey sticks" were sighted "beating a ball." And sometimes the results were disastrous. "What game are they playing?" asked young Thomas in this book published in England in 1813. "It is called hockey," replied a Mr. White. "It was a favourite game when I was a boy at school but it was put a stop to by a very melancholy accident when a teacher was struck in the eye by a stick and lost an eye."

"Field hockey was played 'in some form or other' in the early days of the 19th century," wrote the author of *Hockey for Men and Women* in 1955. "Goals were a formed of an arch made of long pieces of bent briarwood. The sticks were cut from

This Roman frieze, discovered in the 16th century, shows two streakers "bullying" for a ball, as in modern field hockey face-offs.

Short sticks — less than three feet long — forced most field hockeyists to play one-handed.

branches of trees and hedgerows with large knobs at one end. The ball was made of wood or cork, bound with string and called 'the hockey.'"

A version of "this fine old English game" was played on a large meadow or open common with a wooden ball or "ordinary cask bung." Players were required to strike "from right to left" or be subject to suspension from play, reported *The Sports and Pastimes of American Boys"* in 1884. At times the ball was called the hockey, at other times the stick was given this name. "The shape and dimensions of the hockey stick are entirely arbitrary, being left to the peculiar taste of the owners. Some like their hockeys to be sharply hooked, while others prefer them merely bent in order to neutralize the blows of the opposite side, while others can play best with a slight and springy weapon, that can be used with one hand."

The Reverend Mr. A.E. Bevan, recalling the days of 20-aside hockey in the early 1800s, noted that a rubber ball was "cut in angles all around" so that it would not bounce equally. "There was no limit to the field of play, except as far as the goal line was concerned. Should a player come in on the wrong side [i.e., the left side] as you were dribbling [stick-handling] down, you were at liberty to hit him across the shins."

Lord Lytton (1803-1873), an English novelist and politician, described field hockey in 1853 as "an old fashioned game" that was preserved in the primitive vicinity of Rood by young men and farmers. A graduate of Trinity College, Cambridge, Lytton described hockey as "very uncommon in England except at schools." In the 1860s field hockey began to take on a definite shape, *Chamber's Encyclopedia* reported a century later: "As there was no limit to the playing field goals could be scored from anywhere (the striking circle came later) and players tackling on the left side could be hit over the shins."

In Elizabethan times in England, hockey was played on any level surface — the first road hockey game!

There were different versions of the game, depending on where one lived. In Blackheath, southeast of London, where the first Football and Hockey club was formed in 1861, oak sticks were bent by steam, and both sides of the flat back could be used to hit the ball. This club recorded the first 15-aside game: one goalkeeper, two backs, two three-quarter backs, three halfbacks, and seven forwards, which was similar to rugby football.

By 1868, Eton College's version of the rules limited the sides to 11 players each. A key rule stipulated that "the stick must be held on the right side of the player and the ball struck with it in that position, in order that all collision of bodies and roughing be avoided." Any player violating this rule and impedes his adversary can "with impunity be struck on the shin."

Published in the *College Chronicle*, the 30 rules of the game recommended a ground 300 by 150 feet and goals 20 feet wide and seven feet high.

The bully or face-off carefully stipulated that each side be drawn up in a long line in the direction of the length of the ground "having their right hands towards their own goals." No player was allowed to raise his stick above his knees, except in the Lamming Sticks area (20 yards out from the goal line), where he could "hit it as hard as he likes."

The first field hockey governing body was formed in 1875 – coincidentally, the same year that ice hockey was first played under similar field hockey rules in Canada. The Hockey Association in England rejected the Blackheath code, advocated the use of a cricket ball, and adopted football characteristics of passing and shooting, including the all-important offside rule—no forward passing. When the association reorganized in 1886, the rules adopted were based on Wimbledon's, but included some from East Surrey. The goals were limited to two uprights 12 feet apart, with a horizontal bar or tape seven feet from the ground.

Women turned the demur field game into a dashing sport.

This face-less hockey figure or golfer has been portrayed in cut glass in England's Gloucester Cathedral since 1850.

By 1810, young boys used crude sticks to duel for a circular object.

Early field hockey games were more of a free-for-all melee with opposing sides using inverted canes to battle for a ball. An artist drew this scene about 1864.

Queen Victoria's son, Prince Albert Victor, loved polo, polished his hockey skills in the British Army, toured Canada as Lord Renfrew and became the first president of the new (Field) Hockey Association in 1886. Punch *portrayed him playing the game in 1863.*

The "bully" was explained thusly: "Each player is to strike the ground on his own side of the ball, and his opponent's stick over the ball three times, alternately, after which either of the two players shall be at liberty to strike the ball." The offside rule pointed out that when a player hits the ball, "anyone of the same side who at the moment of hitting is nearer his opponent's goal line is out of play and may not touch the ball himself."

Field hockey, once described as "a crude stick game," had, in a space of 11 years, reduced the number of rules from 30 to 19 and produced a more scientific action that would be followed on grass and ice throughout the world. Hockey, which once accepted 'shinning', was too good a game, said historian Miroy, "to remain a rough and tumble."

Peter Moss summed up the progress succinctly in *Sports and Pastimes Through the Ages,* published in 1962: "Rules were gradually added, overhauled, and amended so that by the end of the century, instead of the murderous brawl it had been 50 years earlier, hockey was considered fit even for young ladies to play." In days before mass participation of females in all sports, some "Hockey Girls" were cited for "their athleticism and fresh good looks." Today, field hockey is largely played by females throughout the world.

The English field game, however, did not always impress Canadians who had seen only one activity played by males on ice. "I saw a hockey game ... played by girls," Harold W. Price, a Canadian soldier, wrote in his diary during the First World War. "It is played with crooked sticks more like bludgeons ... and with a cricket ball. It is played like association football [soccer] and nothing at all like our [ice] hockey. Deliver me from English hockey!"

HOCKEY.

Upraised sticks were symbolic of field hockey games captured by 19th century artists.

Street hockey battles, according to this ornate engraving, were popular in Merry England in the early 19th century.

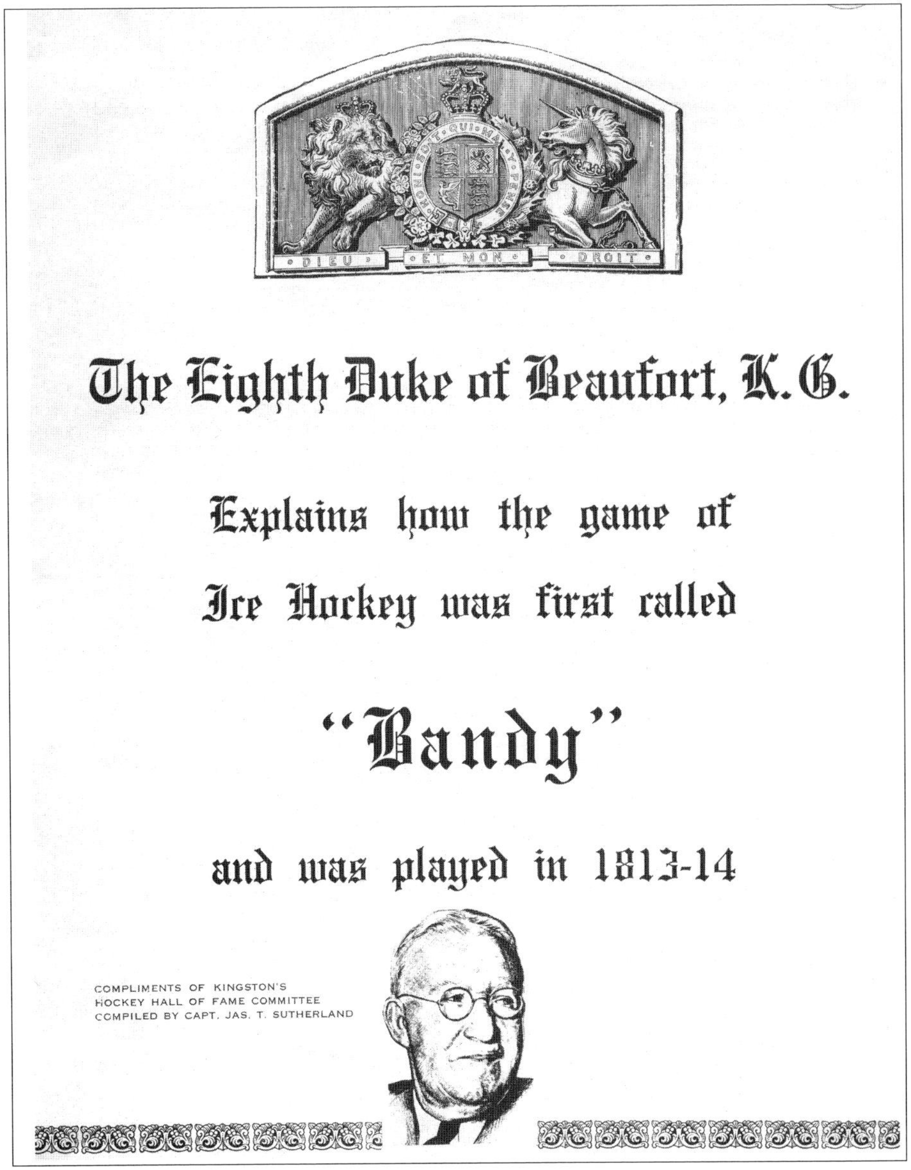

DIEU ET MON DROIT

The Eighth Duke of Beaufort, K.G.

Explains how the game of Ice Hockey was first called

"Bandy"

and was played in 1813-14

COMPLIMENTS OF KINGSTON'S
HOCKEY HALL OF FAME COMMITTEE
COMPILED BY CAPT. JAS. T. SUTHERLAND

Bandy's close association with ice hockey was first documented by Canada's Capt. James T. Sutherland in the 1940s, when the origin of the game was under study. Bandy was first played in England as early as 1813–14.

English field hockey sticks had to be hardy enough to hit a cricket ball. Eleven-man sides were positioned similar to early football teams.

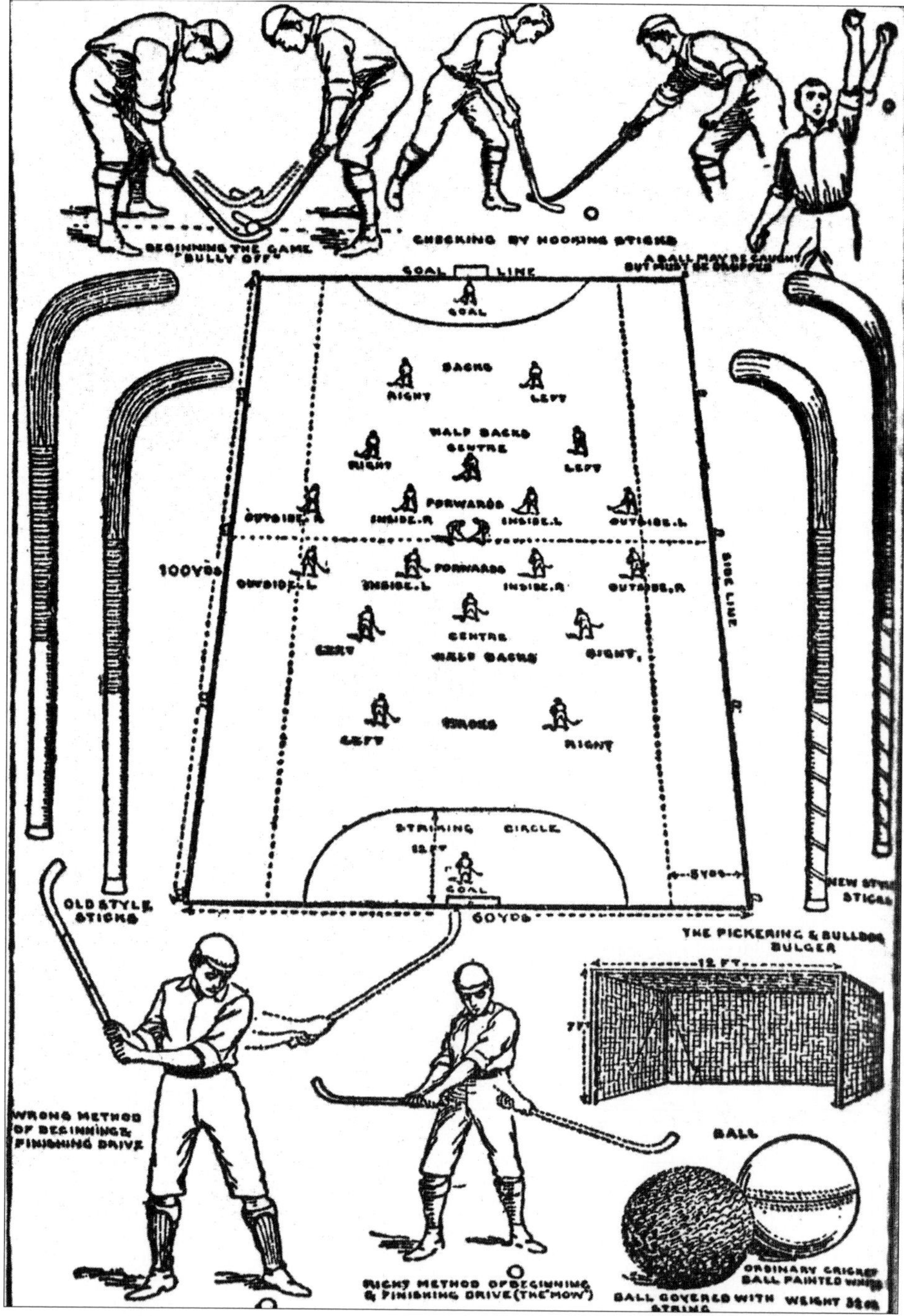

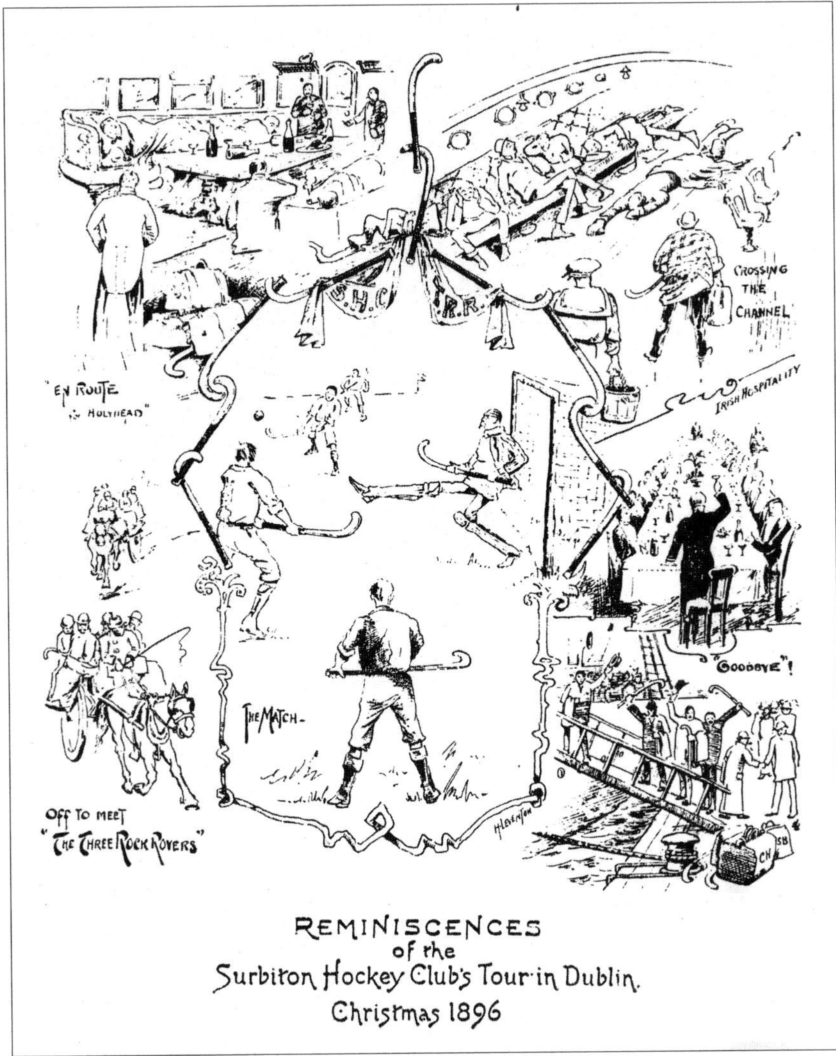

By 1896, artists were illustrating the joys of overseas hockey tours — to Ireland.

More than sticks clashed in schoolboy matches in Britain in the early 20th century.

> "Had freezing cold spells in England not been punctuated with warming spells, ice hockey probably would have become a distinctively English, rather than Canadian game."
>
> —William J. Baker, *Sports in The Western World,* 1982.

CHAPTER 7
Hockey-on-the-Ice
My favourite game!

Although born and bred Canadians rarely refer to their national winter sport as "ice hockey," there is another game that was an important link in the transition of field hockey to gleaming ice and the development of the game in Canada. That is "hockey-on-the-ice" or field hockey transferred to a frozen surface, a much different game from what most non-observers refer to as "ice hockey" today.

Hockey-on-the-ice originated in England, some calling it bandy. "Hockey on the ice is the counterpart to bandy on terra firma, the method of the two games being substantially the same," Norman and Albert Goodman stated in *Fen Skating*. It was published about 1882 when Canadians had already formulated a seven-man, onside, ice game simply called hockey.

The first written use of the six-letter word 'hockey' in North America occurred in Canada's far north in 1825. British naval lieutenant John Franklin, during his second expedition in the Mackenzie River region, reported his men took part in the old field game on the Arctic ice as a recreational exercise. Playing stick-ball field games on any level, frozen surface was common in the nineteenth century. "Till the snow fell the game of hockey played on the ice was the morning's sport," the future Sir John wrote to geologist Roderick Murchison in November 1825. His recorded words contained no specific details as to what the Royal Navy crew members wore on their feet. However, a later entry in Franklin's dairy indicated that his men had enjoyed "amusements of skating and the evening games on the ice." These words, Ottawa journalist Randy Boswell concluded in 2003, were interpreted to mean that they were engaged in a bona fide version of ice hockey. But there is no unmistakable, first-hand evidence to

On the frozen Thames River at Richmond, England, men in top hats wield sticks in their right hands, as required in field hockey.

British women skaters did not let long skirts deter them from trying hockey-on-the-ice at Wimbledon in the late 19th century. Note the movable goal posts.

Queen Victoria, in an "elegant sled" pushed by Prince Albert, viewed one of the first field hockey games on ice in the 1850s. The prince, a strong skater, organized hockey games for members of the Royal household at Frogmore House, Windsor, England.

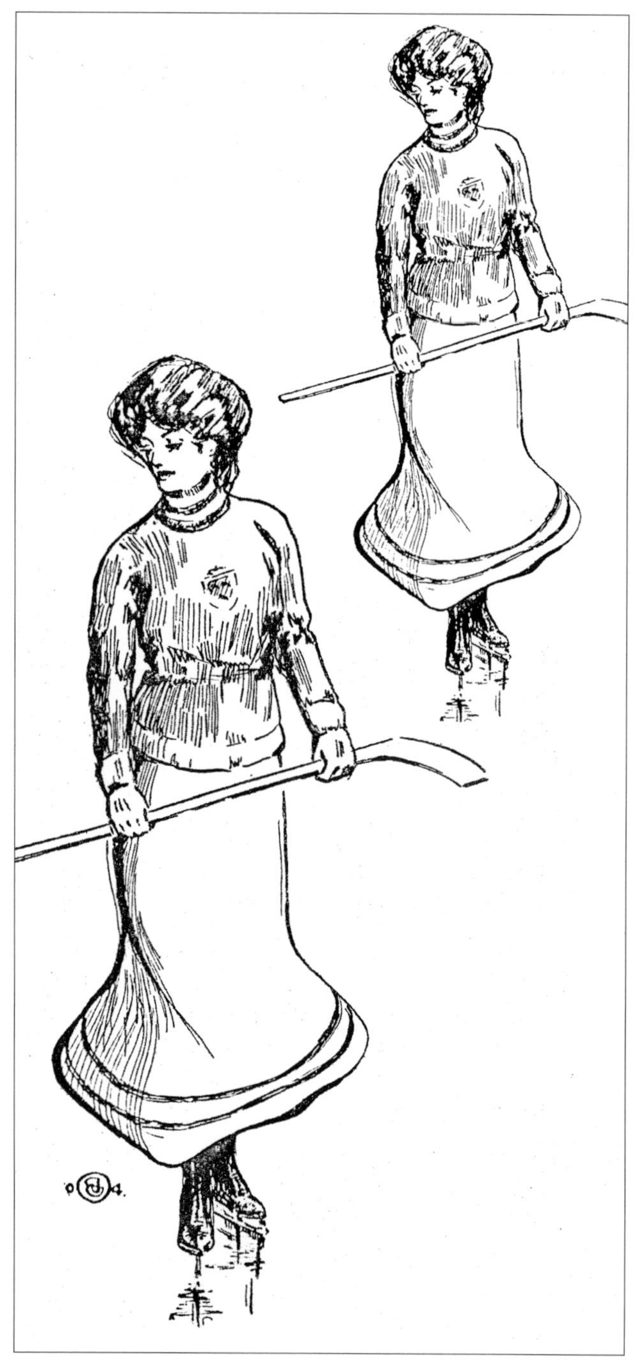

McGill University lassies, in high pompadours, showed only their ankles in early 1900 games.

show that skates were worn when hockey was played on the ice. The jury is still out.

Hockey players on ice skates, however, were observed 18 years later by a British army officer stationed in Kingston, Upper Canada. In 1843, Arthur Freeling, a 22-year-old lieutenant with the Royal Engineers wrote in his diary: "Began to skate this year, improved greatly and had great fun at hockey on the ice." One historian, studying this sentence, said it could not be assumed that Freeling was wearing skates when he played hockey on the ice, but that is clearly the inference. Freeling, a product of Harrow College, Middlesex, where organized field hockey was in its formative stage, was one of several British officers and aristocrats who had used skates, stick, and ball in rare opportunities on a frozen surface in their native island and practiced it in their adopted home. This Canadian garrison town, at the confluence of the Cataraqui River, Lake Ontario and, the St. Lawrence River, had previously recorded only the activities of the large Scottish community playing annual games of shinty, the rousing Highland field game. Decades later, a Kingston diarist recorded details of boys on blades playing "shinny" on the

The farming community turned out en masse *for this more formalized version of hockey on the ice near Olds, Alberta in the 1920s.*

harbour ice where Freeling first enjoyed stick-ball action.

Hockey-on-the-ice could truly have been said to have regal approval as the game was launched early in the Victorian era. In 1850, Prince Consort Albert, husband of Queen Victoria, was considered "a fine shot," played skittles, exercised on bicycles, played indoor tennis, and skated well. "When the frost held he organized ice-hockey matches with members of the Household," Joanna Richardson reported in *Victoria and Albert*, published in 1977. In 1853, members of the British Royal Family transferred the field game to ice, noted Ian Gordon in *The History of Hockey*: "Sides were chosen, sticks found and a wooden plug or stopper pried from a barrel was used as a puck." Maybe the first non-ball "puck" on ice!

A noted British sportsman, John Dugdale Astley, later knighted (as was Arthur Freeling), played hockey "on fast ice" at Oxford University. He recorded another case of early British hockey on the ice at the outbreak of the Crimea War. "Just previous to Christmas we had a lot of hard weather, and with it some first-rate ice, which gave me ample opportunity of playing my favourite game of hockey on the ice," he recalled in his 1894 book, *Fifty Years of My Life*. "I don't think that I ever enjoyed a game more ... The game waxed fast and furious and I am afraid that I was sufficiently wanting in respect to interference, at least, with the Prince Consort's equilibrium in my eagerness to get a goal."

The Royal game was not an isolated affair. Eleven years later in 1864, when the royal couple were staying at the royal residence, Frogmore House, Windsor, the weather turned cold. Albert

Hockey-on-the-ice — field hockey moved to a frozen surface — is reproduced from a scene engraved on a Kingston, Ontario trophy made in England.

American artist C.J. Taylor depicts the rudimentary sticks and lively action of hockey-on-the-ice, sketched in 1884.

Hockey at Hengler's rink by English artist Ernest Prater depicts the transition of field hockey and bandy to indoor artificial ice in 1896. Note players wielding slim, field hockey sticks are shooting both right and left. Figure skaters (left) were part of the night's program.

Budding shinny or polo players had to run the gamut of skate-chairs and sleds in early games on frozen ponds in New England. They carried curved sticks from tree branches.

or "Bertie," then the Prince of Wales, drove to Virginia Water, where ice had formed on an artificial lake within the grounds of Windsor Great Park. The Prince organized a game of ice hockey, while his daughter, Alexandra, the newly married Princess Royal, was pushed about the ice in a chair fitted with runners, similar to the one on which Albert had propelled Victoria a few years earlier.

While the sun shone and a band played, Alexandra complained of slight birth pains and returned to the house. "Lady Macclesfield look worried," wrote David Duff in *Alexandra: Princess and Queen,* 1980, "but Bertie pooh-poohed her fears and went on with his game." And his wife went on with the birthing. Albert Edward, later the Duke of Clarence, was born January 14, 1864.

Early hockey in England was very much a one-handed game because of the short sticks.

He played field hockey at Royal Military College, Sandhurst, and became the first president of The Hockey Association, when the field hockey organization was reorganized in 1886.

By the 1860s, the hockey-on-the-ice pastime had reached another North American city — Halifax, Nova Scotia — where another stick-ball game had held forth for decades. "Garrison and Fleet played hockey at one end of Oathill Lake and young men from Dartmouth and city were playing two well-contested games of ricket," said *The Halifax Reporter* in February 1867, five months before the Atlantic province joined the new confederation of Canada.

Haligonians, already familiar with wicket or ricket, a game based on the Irish field game of hurling, were barely familiar with this new game of "hockey." In 1864, T*he Halifax Reporter* noted that boys had abandoned stone-throwing for "hockey on the ice," but resorted to mimicking those who were not "quite at home on skates."

On January 25, 1864, another newspaper, *The Halifax Morning Sun,* reprinted an 1862 warning from a British newspaper that some Nova Scotian

Games played on the St. Lawrence River in front of the Bonsecours Market building in Montreal in the 1880s were described as "hockey-on-the-ice." Note the goal posts.

newspapers and historians claimed as their own: "Hockey is a noble game ... but on ice it is in its wrong place. It is impossible to enforce the rules in such a miscellaneous assembly ... and anyone who happens to have a stick hits the ball in any direction."

Thirty years later, the "hockey-on-the-ice" phrase was still common in England as the National Skating Palace (Hengler's) showcased the game just off Oxford Circus in central London. "Hockey on the ice has always been a favourite sport with good skaters," *Black and White Magazine* reported in its April 4, 1896 edition. The sport, thanks to artificial ice, "could be enjoyed by performers and witnessed in complete comfort by spectators." An accompanying illustration, reproduced in Martin Harris's *Homes of British Ice Hockey* (2005), showed players with bandy-type sticks pursuing a round puck. The regulations governing play were not elaborated on.

The codification of ice hockey rules occurred a decade later, 1,000 miles away in another city, Montreal, Quebec. In 1876, when the first rules were printed in Montreal's *Gazette*, they were identical with those of field hockey, except for the word "ice" replacing "field." The news report, headlined as "Hockey on the Ice," pointed out that the game was played indoors at Victoria Skating Rink under "Hockey Association" rules. Strangely enough, another code, referred to as "The Halifax Hockey Club Rules," which permitted forwarded passes, was briefly cited as the style for the early games in Montreal but never adopted. (An interpretation of "The Halifax Rules," based on a Nova Scotia report first printed in Boston in 1859, was published in *The Puck Starts Here* in 1996. Twelve in number, including four rules from modern hockey, they were summarized by author Garth Vaughan, a retired surgeon who has mythologized Windsor, N.S. as the birthplace of hockey.

Europeans had their own ideas as to how the game should be played. They did not completely follow the Canadian code. In 1912, two years after the formation of the International Ice Hockey Federation, the version of the game in Europe astonished one Canadian commentator. "To start off, they allow the forward pass ... the length of the ice," scoffed an *Ottawa Journal* columnist. "Then they have a 'crease' in front of the goal nets inside of which no goal may be scored." The rules debate was off and running!

Two natilly-dressed lads swing inverted canes at a large ball on the ice in this 19th century illustration, suggesting that field hockey and shinty were first played on ice without skates.

When Britains moved the game indoors with a puck in 1895, an artist illustrated the first Canada-England contest in front of a fashionable audience.

> "Young men of the city [of Halifax] are second to none in the world for energy, skill and daring in all manly games."
>
> —*The British Colonist,* 1859

CHAPTER 6
Wicket or Ricket
The spirit-stirring game

The Atlantic Provinces, being the closest North American land to Europe, were in a prime position to be innovators in the introduction of nineteenth-century sport and folk pastimes. Their salt water harbours did not freeze as fast as lakes and streams in the interior, but despite a more moderate climate, Maritime ponds and nearby lakes provided surfaces for skaters pioneering in stick-ball games.

All the nineteenth-century folk recreations practiced on field or ice in North America had their roots in Scotland, England, or Wales through shinty, bandy, and field hockey. In Nova Scotia and Newfoundland, another culture spawned its earliest game on ice. Because of its influx of Irish immigrants in the 1800s, the stick-ball game played on the East coast showed the influence of Eire's field game of hurling. Strangely enough, the name of the game closely resembled the name of the English game of cricket. It was called "wicket," describing the goal which the cricketer defended against the bowler. In later years, the Halifax game was known as ricket — "cricket" without the letter "c."

The connection with the Irish field game was first cited in Halifax's *Acadian Magazine* in the summer of 1827. Tim Fashion, in a poem entitled "Winter — Now," penned the words: "Now at ricket with hurlies some dozens of boys / Chase the ball o'er the ice, with deafening noise." Credit for this revelation goes to author-researcher, the late Leslie S. Loomer in his 1996 publication, *Windsor, Nova Scotia: A Journey in History.*

Irish labourers, employed on the construction of the Shubenacadie Canal linking Dartmouth and the Minas Basin, spent their leisure hours with hurley sticks in hand, pursuing an object on the ground. This version of the field game, played

Wicket and ricket, as played in Halifax-Dartmouth, Nova Scotia, were names derived from the English game of cricket. Cricketers defended wickets (two sticks) and ricket players called their goals "wickets."

Cricket bats in the 1800s were curved like hockey sticks to hits balls pitched underhand.

by any number of men or boys in Ireland, was recorded as "hurly on skates" by a Pictou, Nova Scotia newspaper editor in 1829. In the era before shin pads and thick catalogues, he called it "the delectable game of break shins."

Two years later in Halifax's North West Arm, a team from the town and one from the military faced each other in "the spirit-stirring game of wicket." By 1842, on Maynard's Lake across Halifax Harbour near Dartmouth, the match was referred to as "ricket" with no explanation of the action.

In 1844, novelist Thomas Chandler Haliburton, the creator of the fictional "Sam Slick," made a reference to schoolboys with hurlies playing a game on a long pond. One hundred and fifty years later, residents of Haliburton's hometown, Windsor, Nova Scotia — despite any reference to skates — seized upon this skimpy reference to the ice action in the book of fiction (*The Attache)* and created their own birthplace of hockey myth. This attempt illustrates the definition of myth put forth by the distinguished Canadian historian Arthur R.M. Lower: "Myth establishes its own version of history, partly by colouring of fact, partly by the deliberate suppression of unwelcome facts." The

Skaters outnumbered hurley players on the ice at North West Arm in Halifax, Nova Scotia, in this 19th century scene.

THE RULES OF RICKET OR WICKET

(as recorded in the Boston Evening Gazette, November 1859) and reported played in Halifax, N.S., 1831-1875).

1. *The rickets, or goals, consist of two cobble stones formed at one distance from one another.*
2. *The sides are formed by two persons tossing or drawing lots for first choice of partners...until a sufficient number is obtained on each side.*
3. *Any number may play—"the more the merrier."*
4. *Each ricketer is provided with a hurley (stick.)*
5. *All being ready, a ball is thrown in the air.*
6. *A ricket (goal) is chosen by each side and placed in charge of a man whose duty it is to prevent the ball from passing through.*
7. *The game may be 10, 15 or 20, or any number agreed upon, the side counting the number first being winners.*
8. *The counting consists in putting the ball through your adversary's ricket (goal), each time counting one.*
9. *From the moment the ball touches the ice...it must not be taken in hand...but must be carried or struck about the ice with the hurlies.*
10. *Whenever the ball is put through the ricket (goal) a shout "game ho!" resounds from shore to shore.*

Curling was in the forefront of games played on the Dartmouth lakes near Halifax, but skaters with curved sticks or "hurleys" played rickets (right), while British soldiers and sailors indulged in "hockey." This scene was sketched by a British officer in the 1860s.

Windsor birthplace claim was refuted by the Society for International Hockey Research after a year-long study and report in 2002. "Fiction by its very nature," wrote Gerald Tomlinson, author of *The Baseball Research Handbook* (1987), is NOT a research source."

The ambitious town on the edge of the Annapolis Valley could muster only one other report of "hurley" or "ricket" being played there, and the town's earliest mention of its first game of organized "hockey" was 44 years away (1888). In Halifax, 40 miles east of Windsor, it was just the opposite. In every decade the local press recorded some ice games, and the sticks reported were "hurlies" as used in hurling.

By 1859, there was a detailed explanation of "the favourite game in Nova Scotia." *The British Colonist* explained that two "rickets" or stones "about as large as cobblestones" are placed three or four feet apart and frozen to the ice, and the playing surface extended according to the number of players. Sides — "the more the merrier"— were formed by two persons tossing or drawing lots and selecting alternately, as done in school-yard or playground pick-up games today.

A ricket game was started by a designated player or independent person tossing a ball in the air—as is done to commence hurley or the Scottish field game of shinty. The team putting the ball through the adversary's wicket "10, 15 or 20 times" was declared the winner.

"From the moment the ball touches the ice," said *The Colonist* in 1859, "it must not be taken in the hand ... but must be *carried* or struck about the ice with the hurlies." Carrying the ball on the face of the broad-bladed hurley stick was a feature of Irish hurling. It is much more an aerial game than field hockey, which is confined to ground or ice but spiced by long lifting.

The two games, field hockey on the ice and the Nova Scotian version of hurling, came under "study" in Canada's Confederation Year, 1867. A few months before Nova Scotians somewhat reluctantly voted to join the Canadian union of provinces, Haligonians could view the officers of the garrison and the Royal Navy "in a match called hockey," while Halifax and Dartmouth skaters "followed up the ball" with their hurlies in a game of "ricket."

"Very little science was displayed in either game," reported *The Halifax Reporter*. "The old class of players seem to have died out and their successors are not in the science of leading off the ball, doubling (stick-handling) and carrying it through."

Two years later in 1869, the *Acadian Recorder* reported that a ricket club was to be formed in Halifax to play "the interesting winter sport of ricket." Although a highland regiment, a cricket club, and a Dartmouth team were interested in organizing a ricket competition, it was the Young Haligonian club that formed an executive and

The Maritime game and the Montreal style of hockey clashed in 1889, when a Dartmouth team first played exhibition games in Quebec province. Kingston artist Frank Edwards sketched this version of the Nova Scotia team in Montreal's Victoria Skating Rink. Note the curling stones placed parallel to the sides of the rink to eliminate scores on long shots.

appointed a captain. Apparently, the proposed league never reached fruition. No formal matches were ever recorded in the press. Maybe the weatherman intervened — the winters following (1870) were mild, and colder weather to the west was to influence the future of organized and codified ice games in a protected environment.

Twenty years later in 1890, Nova Scotians were still playing a variety of ricket when Dartmouth Chebuctos ventured 600 rail miles westward to Quebec City and Montreal, there introducing their version of "hockey." They lost all four games under the free-wheeling Halifax style and under the onside Montreal rules. They soon thereafter adopted the Montreal game and even switched to "forward" for the name of their attackers in place of "rushers," as borrowed from the new but short-lived roller and ice game in the United States.

Modern day observers saw little difference between the various games. One who held that view was Nova Scotian author L.S. Loomer, who supported Windsor's birthplace claims. "The game," he wrote in 1996, "had changed through a whole metamorphosis of names including ricket, shinty and breakshins and had settled down to be ice hockey." But there were other games in other places under other names.

Lateral passing was a special feature of the Montreal game. In contrast the Maritime style permitted forward passing.

Sticks were well taped and caps were a necessity for this line-up of players on a farm pond near Kelsey, Alberta.

> "There is a vast difference in the two games — ice hockey and ice polo — though in the object sought there is a great similarity."
>
> — J.A. Tuthill, *Ice Hockey and Ice Polo Guide,* 1898

CHAPTER 9

Ice Polo

A more open game

If Canadians had not created the organized game of ice hockey, the honour would probably have gone to their neighbours to the south. Some anonymous Americans invented the game of ice polo, based on roller polo, the latter derived from the original polo or "hockey on horseback." New Englanders conceived ice polo well after Canadian hockey was under way, and it fell victim to a superior game developed by its northern neighbour. "Although this game has been largely indulged in, in the past winters, it is believed to be on the decline, due to the rapid increase of a much more scientific game of ice hockey," reported the *Ice Hockey and Ice Polo Guide* in 1898.

Early America, colonized with a similar British mix of people who came later to the northern half of the continent, did not have to search for a stick-ball game. It was already part of their sports or recreational activities. The roots of ice and roller polo could have grown from the ubiquitous game of shinny — the offshoot of Scottish shinty — but because of the early development of the American colonies, a stick-ball game on ice could have been derived from any one of the pioneer games of Britain or Ireland.

British troops, before fleeing New York in 1783, are reported to have played the Irish field fame of hurling, with skates on ice. And a form of hockey was played in Stoney Brook — now Princeton, New Jersey — during the winter of 1786. Another field game leapt the Atlantic to the New World, as cited in the 1989 Colonial Williamsburg book, *Colonial Virginians at Play.* "The national, manly and innocent game of bandy ought not to be suppressed by officers or police," noted the *Norfolk Herald* of 1802 in a tongue-in-cheek reference to the dangerous consequences of the game. "The loss of an eye now and then by the

Canadian ice hockey and American ice polo melded at Turkey Pond, St. Paul's School, Concord, New Hampshire, in the late 1890s. Students of St. Paul's School pioneered an American version of the Canadian game. Note the different shaped sticks.

Hockey was described as "polo" when illustrated in a Canadian magazine in 1883. Note the polo caps.

force of a ball helps the (medical) faculty a little, as sickly season is over; and the panes of glass that are broken put a few dollars in the pockets of the glazier. All trades must live and the practice of bandy, it is hoped will be tolerated."

Years later, in 1839, New England author Jacob Abbott pointed out: "A good hawkey is a great prize to a Boston boy." In the book, *Caleb in Town,* he described "a hawkey" as a small, round stick about as long as a man's cane with crook in the lower end." It was ideal for a boy wishing to hit a little stone on the ground. Noted American naturalist Henry David Thoreau reported that "hawkie" was played "all over the State of Massachusetts" in 1854.

It is no surprise that St. Paul's, an elite boarding school in Concord, New Hampshire, played a combination version of shinny and hockey as early as 1860. An account in the school newspaper, *Horae Scholasticae,* explained play similar to shinny without goals. "One boy swings his hockey and away goes the ball skimming over the ice. The party dashes off in pursuit ... the head boy catches up .. .and sends himself sprawling over the ice on all fours ... the next boy ... sends the ball back again."

Concord is less than 70 miles from Boston, where John L. Shorey, published *Nursery,* "a monthly magazine for youngest readers" in 1874. A poem, entitled "Making a Day of It," clearly indicated the youth of the day enjoyed a stick-ball game: "All are free from school to-day, Huzza! Boys and girls, come out to play! Huzza! Drop your books, and quit your slates, get your hockeys [sticks], sleds and skates: He will miss the fun, who waits, Huzza!"

In 1875, the Concord schoolboys created and published their own "hockey" rules (eight in number), independent of the field hockey rules adopted to ice in Montreal at the same time. Rule

When ice hockey was first introduced as an organized game to Kingston, Ontario, in 1886, the local roller polo club members lent the local players their narrow sticks. Roller polo was a seven-man game with the captain specially designated.

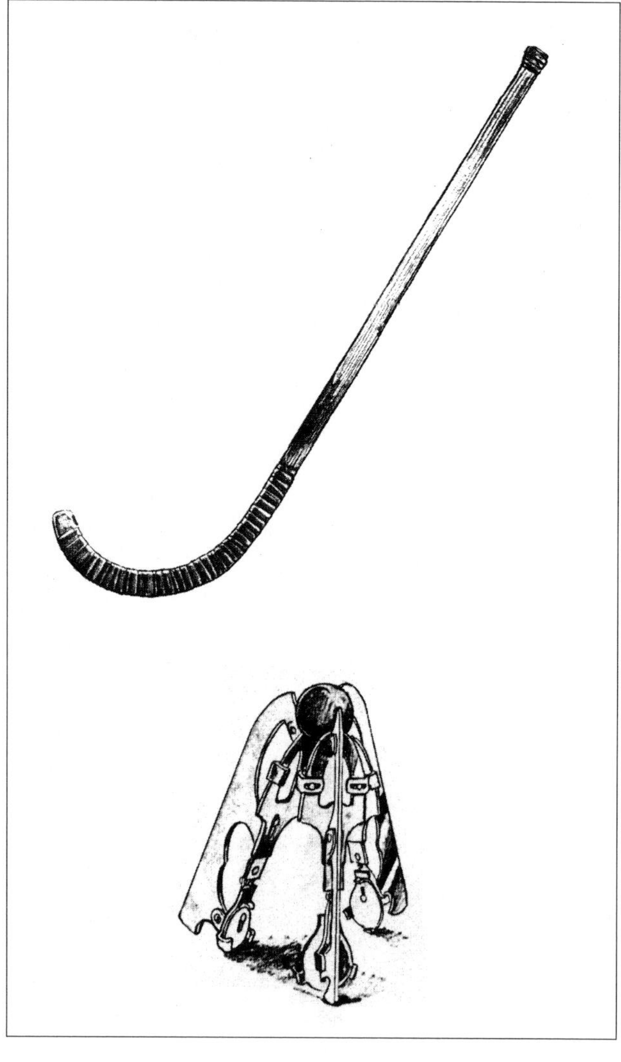

A distinctive curved stick, plus ball and skates, were the necessary accoutrements for ice polo in the New England and mid-western United States.

One limited "the hockey" to no more than five inches in circumference and banned lifting it above the shoulder. The stick wielders pursued a thick, leather-covered base-ball and ruled out "blocks or cricket balls." Players "not on their own side" [ahead of the play] were not allowed to strike the ball. And persistent violators were liable to "expulsion from the game." Eight years later in 1882, the St. Paul's version of hockey reduced the number of players a side from 25 to 11 and added an umpire to officiate disputes. The game was started by a "knock-off from the centre of the field." The object was defined as "a block" and could be advanced by stick or foot.

With such strong hockey roots, how did the polo name and game gain prominence in the United States? Polo, with equestrians wielding wooden mallets, came to North America via India and England in the 1870s. The invention of the modern, four-wheel roller skate was introduced to Newport, Rhode Island in 1866, and a new game sprung forth. According to the *Henley Official Polo Guide*, the early form of the American roller game was "a rough-and-tumble" affair, in which the most muscular team usually came out best. Shades of today's pro hockey before obstruction was called and fighters benched.

Prominent socialites in this exclusive New England community developed roller polo, played with five or six men aside on a 40-foot by 80- foot indoor floor. Each player swung a thin, narrow-

Ice polo, an American game, was an offshoot of roller polo. It was very popular in the New England states in the 1880s and spread to the Midwest.

bladed stick, four feet long, to propel a ball at a goal. "Polo should be played by keeping the ball as much as possible on the surface, not driving it through the air as in shinney or baseball," cautioned the editor of *Henley's Official Polo Guide* in 1886. "Keeping it upon the floor makes a better and more interesting game, and requires more skill, ability and judgment."

Organized roller polo was first played by regular clubs in New England in 1878, three years after ice hockey had been introduced indoors in Montreal. The wheeled game spread to students of the Ivy League colleges of Brown, Harvard, Princeton, and Yale, all of which would have a part in the transition of polo into Canadian ice hockey.

The Massachusetts Polo League was organized in 1884 under stringent regulations to counter the impression that polo games had become "mere exhibitions of slugging and of unpleasant and irritating verbal controversies" between goal judges, referees, and players. Operated in a professional manner under the managers of 14 roller skating rinks, the league resolved one major problem by creating a three by six foot, wire mesh goal and eliminating goal judges . This was 15 years before netting was added to hockey goal posts in Canada. Another advanced innovation was a 3 ?-foot, half-circle goal crease to help protect the goalkeeper.

Six-man teams from teams throughout the state played from November to late May under 32 detailed rules. Unlike early ice hockey, but similar to hurling, forward passing was permitted. The roller poloists teams adopted the face-off from lacrosse and ice hockey, rather than the custom of two centres dashing to the ball in the middle of the floor, and decided games on the best three-out-of five scores. The champions received $700 in medals, plus goal flags or pennants presented by Wright & Ditson, makers of the rubber-covered polo ball.

In the mid-1880s, "polo on skates" moved into roller rinks in central Canada, including Ottawa and Kingston, Ontario, where the narrow polo sticks were borrowed for the introduction of outdoor ice hockey in 1886. However, the American game could not make inroads against the well-established ice game and died with the roller skate craze.

New Hampshire, not Massachusetts, was the leader in the move of the indoor roller sport to a frozen surface. St. Paul's School could well claim to be the first American institution to play a stick-ball game on ice. According to historian Stephen Hardy in a 1997 article entitled "The Making of American Ice Hockey," published *The International Journal of the History of Sport,* the game played at the New Hampshire school called for rules for "hockey on the ice" — the old English pastime, in which errant players could be struck on shins, hands, or head. By 1883, the school had drafted 10 rules, one of which restricted the lifting of the stick above the shoulder. The code also contained

INTERNATIONAL POLO AND HOCKEY TOURNAMENT.

Queen's University,

KINGSTON, ONTARIO,

INTER-COLLEGIATE CHAMPIONS OF CANADA,

VERSUS

Holy Ghost College.

Friday Evening, January 3d, 1896.

Queen's University hockey team from Kingston, Ontario, participated in a joint polo-hockey tournament in Pittsburgh in 1896. After several contests under both rules, the Pennsylvanians adopted the more "scientific" Canadian game.

a vague offside rule by noting that a player "not on his own side" could not interfere with those striking. Violators were subject to expulsion from the game. It was unlike Montreal's first codified rules of 1875 that used 66 words to explain the offside rule and summed it up thusly, "A player must always be on his own side of the ball."

New Hampshire students manipulated "hockeys" in the pursuit of a "block." Years later on the school's Turkey Pond, young males and teachers were photographed, some using hockey sticks and others carrying thin polo sticks. The object of pursuit was not evident.

The big differences between the Canadian and American games were the use of a ball instead of a puck, the use of a one-handed stick, and the absence of any rule prohibiting offside play in ice polo. "Consequently," said the author of an 1898 polo guide, "ice polo is a more open game, the field of players being continually separated and the tries-for-goal being made from passes from unlimited directions."

Recorded references indicate that the transfer of roller polo to ice occurred not in the United States but in Canada. Saint John, New Brunswick, which introduced the American roller skating game to the Maritimes in 1884, made possible the first recorded ice polo games on indoor rinks the following year. Competing teams included tall, muscular Maliseet Indians of the Saint John River valley. Organized ice hockey had yet to arrive in the New Brunswick port, but ice polo had. The transfer of the game across the international boundary may have been instituted through exchanges with fellow game and sea-food hunters among the nearby Passamaquoddy natives of northeastern Maine.

The Micmac-Maliseet Institute of the University of New Brunswick has on record the reminisces of David A. Francis of Pleasant Point, Perry, Maine, whose elders recalled games of ice polo with teams in Saint John, New Brunswick. As a boy, Francis played polo on the ice without skates. "The goals — two rocks set five feet apart — were defended by a goal-tender and a goal-cover who protected the goal-tender," reported Robert M. Leavitt of the M.M. Institute in 1987. "Any number could play but the more players, the longer the game, since the goals were better defended. The first team to score three points won."

Ice polo merged into hockey in New Brunswick, but roller polo rolled westward in the United States. By 1886, it was well established with regular league games in neighbouring Vermont. That winter, the town of Burlington on Lake Champlain invited two noted hockey teams from Montreal to participate in a winter carnival tournament. The host town organized a team of roller polo players to face the winning Canadian team, Crystals, in a game of hockey — the first recorded hockey game in the United States. On the ice of an outdoor slip the teams chased an object, "round one way and

Touring polo teams were ignored by Montreal cartoonists who delighted in portraying novelty matches, such as the "Skeletons vs. Sawed-offs" in Montreal in 1893.

flat the other." American viewers were impressed by the Canadian players' rapid movements and feats of skill.

Five years later in 1891, the New England colleges, including Brown in Providence, Rhode Island, transferred the roller game to outdoor ice and competed in tournaments on frozen ponds in the Boston area. Harvard and Yale universities, Boston and Tufts colleges, and Massachusetts Institute of Technology followed suit before switching to ice hockey.

During the Christmas holidays of 1894-1895, a group of New England ice polo players organized a tour of three Ontario hockey centres —Toronto, Ottawa, Kingston — and Montreal in Quebec. Good individualists but poor combination players, the Americans won two and tied two under polo rules, but were outscored 32-2 under Canadian hockey rules.

Ice polo's last, best season was probably the winter of 1896-1897. Cambridge Ice Polo team, a member of the Massachusetts' league, played an amazing 23 games, mostly exhibitions, against teams stretching from Boston to Brooklyn. They won 22 contests, tied one, scored 121 goals, and gave up only five. In contrast, Montreal Victorias, leaders in the decade-old Amateur Hockey Association of Canada, won the Stanley Cup in their ninth and final game of the year.

Ice polo moved as far west as Wisconsin, where the colder winters made it a popular sport until the mid or late 1890s. Pennsylvania and Maryland, which welcomed the tricolour hockey team of Queen's University of Kingston, Ontario each Christmas, played both games, and spectators in the cities of Pittsburgh and Baltimore "lionized" the Canadian students. The Pittsburgh press described the visitors as being born with skates on feet, and praised the superiority of Canadian hockey over ice polo: "The flat puck ... slips around on the ice much more smoothly than does the polo ball and the rules of the game allow much more scope for teamwork."

As happened in the Maritimes, where the Montreal version of ice hockey took over, the Americans switched to the more scientific, onside Canadian game. Today, it thrives or struggles for prominence in most of the 50 states.

The final word goes to Stephen Hardy, New England's pre-eminent scholar on the American ice game: "Polo set the stage for ice hockey in places like Greater Boston, New York, the Twin Cities, and Michigan's Upper Peninsula. It had all the basic ingredients—lighted indoor rinks, published schedules, skill and violence, heroes, villains, and rabid fan followings. But polo did lack one important product component—'science,' or a sense of team tactics and strategy." Canadian hockey filled that bill.

This dashing attacker adorns the cover of a circa 1900 U.S.A. book on the life of Benjamin Franklin (1706-1790), a century before any ice polo was played. The American statesman's essays included chess and swimming, but no mention of field or ice games.

> "Creighton took a wild, outdoor game played by immigrants and aboriginals and elevated it to one played by gentlemen indoors."
>
> —*Putting a Roof on Winter,*
> Michael McKinley, 2000

CHAPTER 10

Rink Hockey

This fine game!

Until the early 1870s, the play area for stick-ball games was defined by the stretches of available ice and the whims and energies of those who wished to play and to keep the surface clear. The-more-the-merrier "rule" was the order of the day in early games. Teams settled on any number of players, from 10 to 50 or more, for a team. A pioneer described primitive hockey as "a wild but merry scramble" with players using walking sticks, stripped lacrosse clubs, broom handles, or branches of trees.

Concerned with the vagaries of the weather and the necessity of shovelling off a surface, some bright Montrealers moved their recreational games indoors "as often as we could bribe the caretaker of Victoria Skating Rink." This occurred in 1873, one year after a transplanted Maritimer by the name of James George Aylwin Creighton arrived in Montreal and started talking about a game he had seen played in his native Halifax. Two years later, the players of pick-up games, mostly members of skating and football clubs, were ready for a public exhibition, as advertised in a brief public notice in *The Gazette.*

On a Wednesday night, March 3, 1875, two teams of nine players each faced off in a covered, 205 foot by 85 foot ice surface. The game of hockey as we know it had begun.

The next day, *The Montreal Star* reported that the players "excited much merriment as they wheeled and dodged each other and notwithstanding the brilliant play of Captain Torrance's team, Captain Creighton's team carried the day two games [goals] to one." *The Gazette* was a little more detailed in its description of this history making game: "The game is like lacrosse, the block having to go through the flags placed about eight feet apart in the same manner as the rubber ball —

When McGill University hosted Montreal teams on its campus rink, the sideboards were only 6 inches tall and spectators had to clear a spot in the 6-foot high snowbanks.

How-to-shoot was demonstrated by a Canadian artist for the American audience.

but in the main the old country game of shinty gives the best idea of hockey is played, nine aside."

It had taken more than a decade to move hockey under cover of Montreal's palatial skating rink that was built in 1862. Halifax had erected a similar but smaller building the same year, and Kingston followed about the same time, but no one, except the Montrealers, ventured to provide any organized ice action except pleasure and figure skating under their skating rink roof.

The move into confined quarters prompted the invention of a disc to replace the bouncing ball "in order that no accident should happen." The word "puck" — derived from the Irish hurling's word for a "free poke" or shot — was first reported in the Montreal press in 1876. The confined indoor ice rinks, some as small as 150 feet by 58 feet, also sped the reduction of participants, from nine players to eight and then to seven: one goaltender, two defenders, points and cover points, two centremen (one called a "rover"), and two wings.

The next year, in 1877, Montrealers were able to read the printed regulations for this game of hockey on the ice. The seven simple rules differed by only one word – "ice" — from the field hockey rules published in England in 1875. It stipulated that hockey was an "onside" game, with lateral, but no forward, passing.

Eleven years later, in 1886, the first serious codifying of rules of the Canadian ice game was undertaken in Montreal under the game's first formal association. Appropriately, the new Amateur Hockey Association of Canada was first presided over by a full-blooded Mohawk native from Ontario's Grand River Reserve, Thomas D. Greene. A McGill graduate in 1882, he had

McGill University's 1881 seniors posed for Notman photographers at Crystal Palace Rink in what is believed to be the earliest hockey photograph. Nine lightly-clad players made a team.

played in early games for the university, became captain of the Ottawa team, and was cited as "a gentlemanly player and a fine sportsman."

By the time President Greene conducted the first AHA meeting in Montreal, the rules had grown to 16. Some had developed from disputes as a result of keen competition for the first hockey trophy introduced at the Montreal Winter Carnival in 1883.

For the first time the object of pursuit was described. The puck, stipulated Rule No. 11, was to be of vulcanized rubber, "one inch by three inches," as it is to this day. However, the most vital amendment reflected the 'Canadianization' of the game, making it more like the newly organized game of lacrosse and less after British rugby-football. This was effected by Rule 7: When the puck goes off the ice behind the goal it will be considered in play behind the goal line as long as it is on the ice.

In 1889, the first clash of hockey's two solitudes — the hurley dominated Maritimes and the hockey crazy Quebec province — occurred. Dartmouth Chebuctos, the champions of the Halifax district, travelled by rail to Quebec City and Montreal and displayed their particular form of the game. Forward passing was permitted and the goals, marked by curling stones, faced the sides of the rink, which eliminated long shots, but permitted scoring from either side.

When the Montreal game moved to the United States in the mid-1890s, Canadian artists were hired to illustrate "lifting" (icing the puck) and other skills for neophyte New York audiences.

In the mid-1870s James George Aylwin Creighton brought a form of the game played in Halifax, Nova Scotia, to Montreal, Quebec. He captained many Montreal teams and, in the late 1880s, played in the early games in Ottawa, where he served as law clerk to the Senate.

Crude nets designed by Art Ross eliminated some, but not all disputes over goal scoring, according to this 1909 advertisement.

It was much easier for the Montreal players, attuned to the forward passes of their own game of lacrosse, to switch to the Maritime style than vice versa. The Quebec teams dominated under both rules, outscoring the visitors 23 to 3, winning all four exhibition games. The visitors returned to Nova Scotia and soon adopted the Montreal style of game.

The first serious assessment of the new ice game of "Rink Hockey" appeared in written form on the game's 16th birthday in 1891. The article came from the pen of James Macdonald Oxley, a native of Creighton's Halifax, who had moved to Montreal and later lived in Ottawa and Toronto. His ice-breaking article appeared in *Harper's Young People* and later in *The Montreal Daily Star.* A popular literary writer, Oxley provided a succinct summary of the development of the game: "As first played in Canada, hockey went by various names, some of which were apparently merely local — hurley, shinny, rickets — and so forth. It was played only upon the ice in winter-time, and there was not much pretence to rules, each player taking part as best he knew how." No effort was made to systematize the game, Oxley noted, until 1875 when the Montreal Football Club "in search of some lively athletic amusement for the long winter moths, recognized in hockey the very thing they wanted."

By 1889, with many women in attendance for

By 1893, at Montreal's boardless Victoria Skating Rink, a team consisted of seven players. Goaltenders "defended the flags" — two poles stuck in the ice.

A Montreal newspaper artist demonstrates the importance of face-offs and the dire results of "going to the net."

Before the turn of the 20th century, when photo-engraving was perfected, the rousing ice and spectator action was captured by skilled artists. Note the player alignments with defencemen positioned in tandem style, behind two centremen (upper right).

This Febuary 1903 calendar sketch provides a good impression of the rugged, vertical boards in early rinks.

championship games, the Montreal press hailed hockey as "the national winter game of Canada." In 1894, hockey was described as "The King of Winter Sports." Already established for more than a decade in Quebec City and Ottawa, the new game played to enthusiastic crowds in communities within a short radius of Montreal. Kingston, an active shinny centre, took up the formal game in 1886. Toronto followed in 1888. With the establishment of the Ontario Hockey Association 1890, nearly every Upper Canadian town boasted of one or more teams.

The year 1899 was a momentous one for the mecca of hockey — Montreal. The city that printed the first rules also produced the first hockey book, *Hockey: Canada's Royal Winter Game,* written by Arthur Farrell, who would later be inducted into the Hockey Hall of Fame: "Hockey: Fast, furious, brilliant, it is our popular winter sport," proclaimed the star of the Montreal Shamrocks. "Verily it is the game of games … the most fascinating, the most exciting, the most scientific."

In that same year, the good burghers of Mount Royal greeted the opening of the first indoor rink designed for the game. Montreal Arena featured tiered seating and boards around the surface to separate the spectators and the players. Fervent rink-side fans had a habit of getting into the action when players spilled over the low side boards, holding back members of the opposing squad and shoving their own players back into the action.

Money became a major factor as professionalism crept into the Montreal game in the early 1900s. This slate illustration of January 1908 concentrates on the off ice action. The next season, the Eastern Canada league dropped "amateur" from its title.

THE MONTREAL DAILY STAR—TUESDAY, JANUARY 14, 1908.

This 1908 illustration captures the comedy of ice antics and provides a simple view of century-old rink construction — complete with pole obstructions.

WINNIPEG, January 15.—The hockey match on Saturday night, Victorias vs. Winnipegs resulted in six to four in favour of the former team. The whole game was a bitter disappointment to the large audience, and critics are ridiculing the Victorias at the idea of their competing for the Stanley cup. Bain did not play, but watched the game for his own guidance in organizing. The defence is as last year, Merritt, Rod, Flett and Johnstone and is fair. The forward line is weak and lacks combination. Gingras plays in his usual

on Tuesday, the 16th instant. Suital prizes will be presented to the success competitors.

At the Arena on Saturday evening t President's Office defeated the Comptrolle Office before a large gathering of offici and employes of the Canadian Pacific Ra way Company. The score at the call time stood: President's Office, 4; Com troller's Office, 1. The only game scor by the Comptroller's office was while Nels was off the President's team.

Montreal artists dutifully recorded games (scores) and fights in games in 1900. Note the bowler-hatted referee in action.

"Take it all in all, there is perhaps no winter sport exclusively for men that is destined to become more popular, or have more enduring favour," predicted James Macdonald Oxley. "It is safe to say that hockey had definitely taken its place among the national sports of Canada." The *Toronto Mail* in 1880 added this assessment of the new hockey: "For dash, vigour, skill and brilliancy ... there is possibly not its equal anywhere in the world."

In one of the earliest illustrations of outdoor rink action during the 1884 Montreal Winter Carnival, players tried to propel a square puck between unusually high goal posts.

The Lachine Canal, with slanted banks, was an ideal place for hockey games played by Montrealers in the 1890s.

"Shinny is sheer fun, the comedy of ice hockey."
—Doug Beardsley, *Country on Ice*, 1987

CHAPTER II

Shinny Hockey

Sheer fun

While the organized game of rink hockey has continued to develop since that first indoor game in 1873, with rules being codified by hockey associations for amateur and professional play, another game has evolved as a combination of all the folk games we've described. Some aficionados maintain more Canadians of all ages and both sexes play shinny hockey than organized rink hockey.

Shinny hockey is played indoors and outdoors, with or without skates, on ice surfaces, roads, or parking lots, where it goes by different names — pick-up hockey, old-timers hockey, road hockey, street hockey, or boot hockey. The rules are almost non-existent. There are no referees. Everyone is a goal judge. The rare participant is the self-appointed announcer who delights in calling the action as he participates in the play, giving his best impersonation of the legendary Foster Hewitt or current *Hockey Night in Canada* announcer Bob Cole with an ecstatic: "He shoots, he scores!"

Indoors, all the lines and circles of an organized game are ignored except for the centre ice spot for the opening face-off and the goal line. Outdoors, where players are braced by cool Canadian breezes and well aware of varying ice conditions, the only timeouts called are to remove a layer of clothing or to shovel snow off the playing surface. There is no time clock. Which team triumphs is inconsequential. "Next goal wins!" is one game-ending cry.

The only object is sheer enjoyment in skating, passing, checking, shooting, and occasionally scoring. To witness that joy, listen to David Battistella, a National Film Board director, who travelled across Canada, with skates and stick in hand, in the winter of 2000-2001 to record the delights of the simple pastime of shinny in his documentary, *Shinny — The Hockey in All of Us*. Two years later

The joy of shinny on a frozen mill pond is portrayed in this 1943 cartoon.

he called for a National Shinny Day. He calls it "pure hockey" — a game that belongs to all Canadians.

As the Ontario native and his crew filmed shinny sessions at Banff, Alberta, Coppermine, North West Territories, Orangeville, Ontario, Windsor, Nova Scotia, and Canada's capital, Ottawa, he created the "rules" of shinny, published here for the first time:

1. Everyone is a winner.
2. If you want to play, you have to shovel.
3. All pucks are created equal.
4. Shinny is our game; we own it.
5. If Dad builds the rink, the rink gets used.
6. Everyone is welcome and everyone can play.
7. Every puck, every ball, every rock creates its own magic.
8. If you shoot a puck into the snowbank, get it yourself.
9. The Rocket Richard Rule: All players can wear No. 9 in Quebec.
10. In the best shinny games, there are no rules.

Lloyd Davis, a Toronto writer and editor, who is the current secretary of the Society for International Hockey Research, has created a similar document, A CODE OF RULES FOR STREET HOCKEY:

1. To choose up sides, throw everyone's stick into a pile at 'centre ice.' Two captains (usually the oldest kids on the block) take turns selecting stick and throwing them to their respective end of the 'rink.' Wherever your stick lands, that's the team you play for.
2. If you're slow and can't shoot, play 'back'. If you're faster and can shoot, play 'up'. If you brought a baseball mitt — or better still a pair of leg pads fashioned out of old sofa cushions, you're a goalie.
3. No 'risers'— (high shots).
4. Play stops when a motor vehicle approaches. Everyone yells, "Car!" and goal nets are carried to one side of the street. Once the car has passed, everyone yells, "Game on!" and goals are replaced. Play resumes.
5. Common sense dictates how many players are enough for a game. Four are clearly not enough; such a small group should entertain itself by taking shots until sufficient players have arrived on their own or been recruited. Twenty are probably too many, at least on a narrow cul-de-sac.
6. If, in your mind, you visualized yourself as Jarome Iginla, you must 'call it'. This entitles you to the exclusive right to refer to yourself as "Iginla" throughout the game. Unless you call "Iginla," anyone else in the game can pretend he is Iginla, and you'll be left to think of another player.

There's nothing quite like a shinny-hockey game in bracing winter air at an outdoor rink. Cataraqui Conservation Area, near Kingston, Ontario, where scenes for the CBC's historic hockey series were shot in 2004, and Kingston's Victoria Park rink (bottom) are popular spots for students of the game to play without referees and few rules.

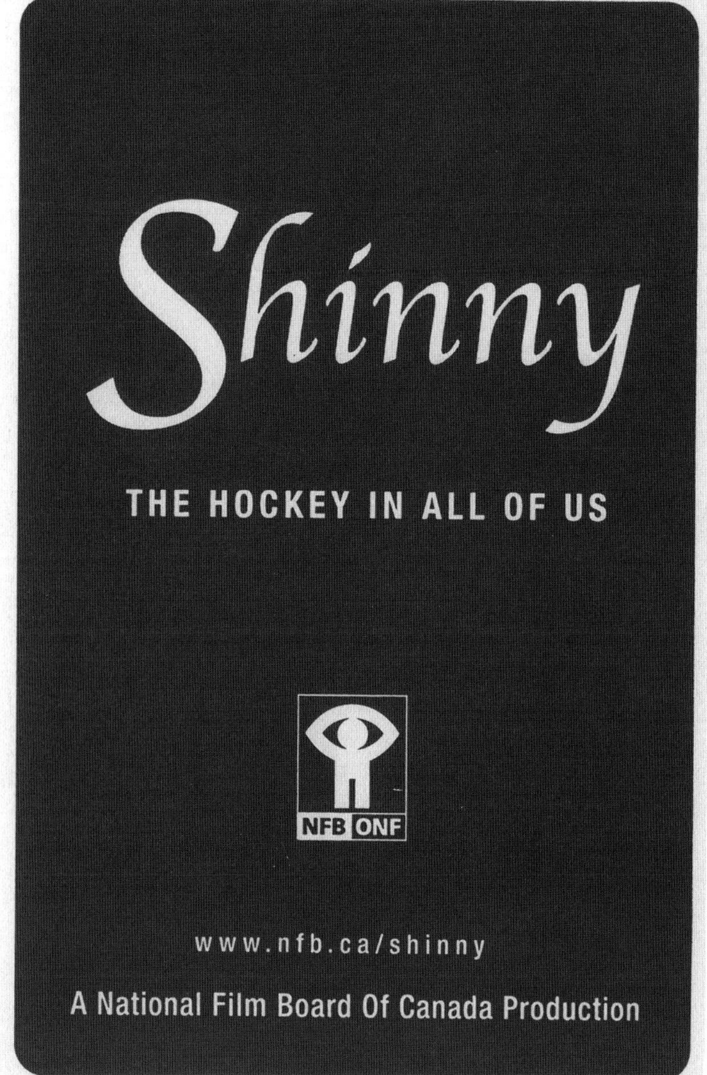

A DOZEN RULES TO LIVE BY

1. Make your own rules
2. You play for fun
3. No fighting
4. Be your own hero
5. No team is ever really beaten
6. All ice is home ice
7. If you want to play, you have to shovel
8. Everyone is welcome
9. If daddy builds the rink, the rink gets used
10. Mother Nature owns the rink
11. Pass the puck
12. Hard work pays off

The informal stick-ball game was saluted by the National Film Board in a 2002 documentary: Shinny – The Hockey in All of Us. *Rules were defined but debatable.*

The ultimate in outdoor rinks, an artificial ice pad, converts Kingston, Ontario's 200-year-old market square into a hockey and skating festival each winter. Three-on-three hockey teams, organized by Kingston natives Doug Gilmour and Kirk Muller, highlight the show. In this match, former Toronto Maple Leaf Wendel Clark chases Hall of Fame defenceman Paul Coffey.

Shinny hockey is an enjoyable way to learn and to improve hockey skills. As Doug Beardsley wryly commented in 1987 with reference to Russian bandy in *Country on Ice*: "The wide-open shinny that results from such a free-flowing contest develops skills of controlling the puck, stickhandling and pinpoint passing occasionally seen in the NHL these days." No wonder coaches, such as former pro Brad Marsh, take midget teams out regularly for relaxing shinny sessions in open-air rinks. Even former Vancouver Canuck and current Los Angeles Kings coach Marc Crawford sees value for professionals in scheduling outdoor shinny practice sessions on game trips to colder climates.

Shiny hockey played indoors or out has its hierarchy – and its "lowerarchy" – according to CBC radio host Tom Allen in his magical book, The Gift of the Game: A Father, a Son and the Wisdom of Hockey. He ranked shinny players from the entry-level Wobbler, through the Digger, Hacker, Clown, Hotshot, and Asshole to the Journeyman. The Journeyman has dekes he never used and is neither young nor old, but is the envy of both."

Holding "formal" shinny games outdoors has become popular in the past few years with well-publicized fun events designed to break the mid-winter blahs. Special tournaments have sprung up from Plaster Rock, New Brunswick and in Canada's capital on the Rideau Canal, the longest skating rink in the world. Fifteen hundred kids on 110 teams played on rinks extending for seven kilometers. In nearby Aylmer, Quebec, tuque-topped youths and helmeted oldtimers "competed" in the first National Capital Pond Hockey Championships. "It truly was a day for celebration, not only how the game is played, but also the way it was," commented Darren Desaulniers of *The Ottawa Citizen* in reporting on the event that was part of CBC's 2004 Hockey Day in Canada.

National Hockey League grads may have sparked the outdoor game craze with a Hockey Classic contest before a record 57,000 fans in frigid weather in Edmonton, Alberta in 2003. The Canadiens-Oilers alumni got a taste of fresh-air shinny with a match that preceded the first NHL outdoor game. However, it was far from traditional shinny. The rink, erected on the football field in The Commonwealth Stadium, was enclosed by regulation boards and Plexiglas, with officials calling offsides and substitutes sitting on heated benches — not standing in chilly snow-banks.

In mid-February 2005, recently retired NHL players Kirk Muller and Doug Gilmour, along with a dozen locked-out colleagues during the NHL players strike, continued the outdoor extravaganza trend, by playing a three-on-three tournament — without rule books or referees — on artificial ice in the historic Market Square at Kingston, Ontario. The weekend Feb-Fest, which

Queen's University students and gentlemen cadets of the Royal Military College of Canada clash annually on the harbour ice in a re-enactment of the first organized game played there in 1886.

included Kingston's 30th Historic Hockey Series, was organized by Muller, who played in the Edmonton game that, he claimed, "showed the innocence of the game." Or as Roy MacGregor reminded us in reviewing the Edmonton classic, "The original purpose of the Canadian game was always FUN."

The beauty of the true outdoor game was succinctly summarized by Ottawa's Stuart Kimmond in a 1993 letter to Canada's national newspaper, *The Globe and Mail*: "Shinny hockey is the sport in it purest form, devoid of aggression, pressure, statistics, equipment, pushy parents and overbearing coaches." Playing this traditional recreational game provides another bonus. "Shinny allows us the great blessing of looking forward to the harshest days of our winters, lets us revel in the fact that we are a winter people," writer Mark James Whaley told *The Globe and Mail* in 1986. "Shinny lets us look back on our own youth when, oh what a lucky time, we played on frozen ponds and streams just outside town."

Shinny in its purist form has attracted men of literature. Doug Beardsley, in his 1987 book, *Country on Ice*, described shinny as "sheer fun — the comedy of ice hockey." Its attraction is "comradeship." That goal remains solidly entrenched today, even sans skates and ice on roads and playgrounds.

May the game never rest in peace but exude joy to every male and female of every age.

A flashback to the good old days: Shinny hockey in its purest form — the comedy of ice hockey.

The anticipatory attraction of shinny-playing city boys to newly-flooded, backyard rinks is captured in a 1914 cartoon.

Ice is not required for road or lane hockey, as illustrated in The Toronto Star.

"It's too bad that hockey can't show us its birth certificate."
— Frank Power, *The Halifax Herald,* 1943

Epilogue

A game for all reasons

So, how did hockey happen? "No doubt," Baz O'Meara wrote in the *Montreal Star* in 1943, "hockey came from a combination of many games," evolving from many stick-ball activities enjoyed over many winters, as we have seen. Let's quickly itemize the contributions of each pastime to Canada's national winter game.

From Native gugahawat (shinny) and lacrosse, for example, came one vital factor in elementary stick-ball games — the goal — two uprights, as opposed to an imaginary line that attackers had to cross in order to score. The traditional "face" or face-off with the puck between the sticks of two facing centremen was introduced from the Canadian game of lacrosse, which dispensed with the native method of throwing a ball up between two or more players. A ball was tossed up between two centre players in Irish hurling. Ditto Scotland's game of shinty. Although the Halifax game of rickets had an aerial feature to commence play, the Montreal organized game of hockey was started with an object placed on the ice.

From hurling came the name of that object – the puck — which makes ice hockey distinctive from any other field or ice game played with a ball. As hockey broadcaster and author Brian McFarlane had the animated character Peter Puck say: "I'm what hockey's all about!" We can say with some certainty that the name of the object that all hockey players covet — the one inch by three inch rubber disk — came from the Irish field game of hurling as "puck" for "free shot." Hockey is the only game that created a distinctive flat disc to pursue. Even English field hockey players slammed around a square of rubber or pursued a round bung of a barrel, not a distinctive, standardized object. It was hockey that put the two together—"round on one side, square on the

The sweet success of field hockey transferred to the ice is portrayed by an European artist. Note all players carry their sticks in their right hands.

other" — after discarding a wooden block.

From shinty came shinny, which ice-endowed Canadians developed into a joyous, recreational form that melded with other games into formal ice hockey. "Hockey is a graduate of Old Man Shinny," *The Daily British Whig* declared in January 21, 1899. Played in the great winter outdoors, shinny still provides a training ground for skaters, passers, and shooters, all important elements for graduates to the game of ice hockey.

Shinny had but one rule —"shinny on your own side" — meaning "play on your own side of the ball or puck," not in advance of the play. That would be offside — a feature of Montreal's hockey game from day one. The onside rule is critical in assessing the vital differences between the free-wheeling folk games of the past and the organized, systemized game of Canadian ice hockey. Montreal created its own style of game based on field hockey and lacrosse rules, playing an onside game, with no passing to a player ahead, whereas the Halifax game of ricket permitted forward passing. James George Aylwin Creighton, who hailed from Halifax, where hockey sticks were called hurleys, had difficulty adapting to the Montreal style and was singled out in the Montreal press for playing offside. Hockey Hall of Fame legend Arthur Farrell, star of the Montreal Shamrocks and author of *Hockey: Canada's Royal Winter Game,* published in Montreal in 1899, said the original Scotch shinty resembled ice hockey more closely than did hurley or English field

Centremen face the sides of the rinks in this illustration from a Montreal magazine of 1893.

Early hockey adopted the field hockey "bully" for a face-off. Facing centres tapped the opponent's stick and the ice three times before jousting for the puck.

hockey. "There can be but little doubt, but that 'shinny,' forerunner of our scientific hockey, is the Canadian interpretation of the game played across the water, adapted in its application to the climate of the country."

Bandy freed participants from the field hockey rule that restricted use of the left side of the stick blade and encouraged the development of stick-handling or dribbling. The English Fen game also pioneered the use of two markers — rocks, snow piles, ice chunks, boots or posts —for defining the width of the goals. Bandy, the game played on the broad icy expanses of the English Fen district, was one of the first recorded stick-ball-skate games, making its debut in the first decade of the 1800s. However, it was eventually eclipsed by field hockey and the transfer of that ancient game to ice, becoming hockey-on-the-ice.

Field hockey was perhaps the greatest contributor to the Canadian game, with the game adapted to hockey-on-the-ice. The original eight rules of Canadian ice hockey were adapted from British field hockey rules. The very name "hockey" was adopted by Montrealers for their new game of ice hockey in the early 1870s. The newly-created Canadian game was started with a "bully," a triple stick-ice tapping custom taken clearly from field hockey. A score of years later, with an assist from Winnipeg teams, the placing of the puck between two facing centres replaced the intricate bully start. Montreal pioneers, however, had made their ice action distinctive from the inception by adopting a completely onside game – no passing to a teammate ahead – as in rugby football. Early bandy didn't enforce any offside rule, but as early as 1875, field hockey introduced an "out of play" rule for those players ahead of the ball.

Games of wicket or ricket, which permitted forward passing, did not influence the onside

The puck, a one-by-three inch disc, separates the Canadian game from all other stick games that use a ball. As Peter Puck, a television cartoon character, said: "I'm what hockey's all about!"

Montreal style of game. However, this Nova Scotia game provided an important root in the early growth of the hockey tree. Ice polo played a belated but significant role in the introduction of American youths to Canadian hockey. Americans played shinny and bandy, but the New Englanders' unique no-offside game of ice polo, a strictly off-side game, came too late to have been involved significantly in the development of Canadian hockey.

Despite the presence of bandy in Russia and Scandinavia today and the Canadians' great love affair with shinny, organized ice hockey continues to grow as a sport in Canada and internationally. Young Russian, Czech, Slovak, Swedish, Finnish, and even Swiss hockey players, let alone Canadian and American kids, long to play in the National Hockey League, the epitome of organized rink hockey. Sometimes too violent at the professional level, hockey is still a vital and vibrant recreational activity for players, officials, and spectators.

A complicated genealogy, to be sure. But the thorny question persists: What is the birth-place of Canada's national winter game? Despite the fact that it is almost impossible to declare a place of birth for a sport that evolved, several communities claim the honour. Windsor, Nova Scotia, Halifax-Dartmouth, Nova Scotia, Montreal, Quebec, and Kingston, Ontario, and even Decline, Northwest Territories, have all been pretenders and contenders for the elusive title.

Windsor latched on to the birthplace logo late in the game. Sparked by celebrations of the 200th anniversary of the founding of King's-Edgehill School there in 1988, "The Little Town of Big Firsts" based its claim on the fictional writing of Sam Slick creator, Thomas Chandler Haliburton, who wrote in *The* Attache in 1844 about school-boys "racin', yelpin', hollerin' and whoopin' like

This stick, used in Kingston in 1888, was similar to a field hockey stick, and the puck, like a lump of coal, was a squared lacrosse ball.

mad" while playing hurly on Long Pond on the ice. The skateless reminiscence was attributed to the early 1800s when Haliburton was a pre-teen student. However, the Windsor birthplace claim was not supported by any other hard evidence, and the Society for International Hockey Research refuted the claim in an 18-page report released in Montreal in 2002. The fervent Windsor supporters have declined to dismantle their highway sign proudly proclaiming the town as hockey's birthplace.

In 2002, Dartmouth lawyer Martin Jones countered the Windsor claim in his well documented book, *Hockey's Home: Halifax-Dartmouth, The Origin of Canada's Game.* Martin's publisher claims he brought forth "an overwhelming, often surprising collection of evidence that points to the two Nova Scotia harbour cities as the true home of hockey in Canada." Jones dismissed Windsor's claim convincingly, but devoted little space to Montreal, where the indoor game was introduced and nurtured, rules defined, and equipment developed, or to Kingston, where the founder of the International Hockey Hall of Fame, Captain James T. Sutherland, declared in 1943, "I think it is generally admitted *and has been substantially proven* that the actual birthplace of organized hockey is the city of Kingston."

The venerable hockey official knew of the Edward Horsey diaries, which documented shinny on Kingston harbour ice in the 1860s, but was unaware of an earlier citation by British army officer Arthur Freeling , who recorded that he learned to skate and play hockey on the ice in January 1843. The organized game with limited rules was not played by Queen's College and Royal Military College cadets in The Limestone City until 1886 — 11 years after Montrealers played their first recorded game indoors in 1875.

In 2003, the hamlet of Deline in the Northwest Territories grabbed the brass ring and 15 days of publicity by maintaining that Sir John Franklin's 1825 diary gave them the honours. The British explorer wrote in his diary: "Till the snow fell the game of hockey played on the ice was the morning's sport." The fact that no skates were mentioned at the time, as was the case with the Windsor claim, did not deter the northerners from maintaining it was a bona fide version of ice hockey. Deline created a web site proclaiming the discovery and inferred that the game was played under "Hudson Bay Rules," an anecdotal term for no-rules shinny.

While Maritimers were leaders in creating an unorganized recreational folk game on outdoor ice and Kingstonians were excited about annual games of shinty on the ice, it was Montrealers, influenced by at least one east coaster (J.G.A. Creighton), who systemized hockey, established a standard playing area, created distinctive uniforms, and initiated annual competitions. Some astute Montrealer selected the game name of hockey —

not hurley, rickets, bandy, or shinny — and started it on the way to becoming an indoor spectacle, Canada's National Winter Sport, a game now popular in northern European and Asiatic countries, where the first stick-ball games originated.

A final word goes to the late Henry H. Roxborough, dean of sports writers, in *One Hundred Not Out* (1966): "Halifax may well have been the source of pioneer hockey. There is equally no doubt that Montreal, because of its experimenting, organizing, legislating and developing is entitled to be recognized as the birthplace of hockey."

Or as my father, English-born J.C. (Jack) Fitsell (1898-1998), who spent half a century making bread (when not flooding a rink for his sons, daughter, and neighbourhood kids) might have said, "Nova Scotians mixed the flour and water, but Quebecers added the yeast that caused it to rise into an attractive baked loaf that Canadians have been slicing, spreading, and savouring for 130 years."

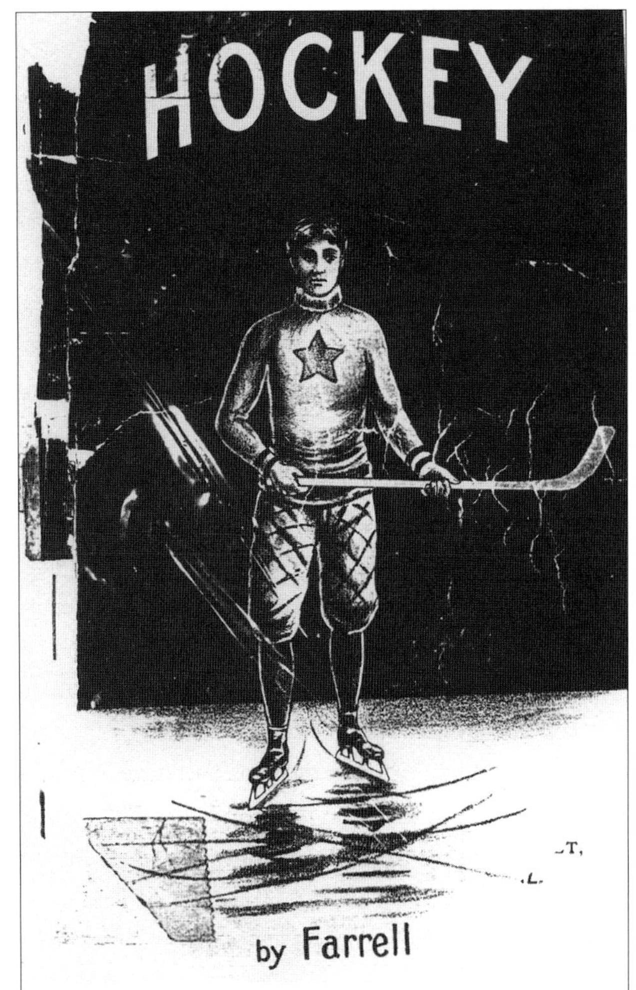

Montreal's Arthur Farrell couldn't fully delineate the ice game's roots when he published the world's first hockey book in 1899. However, the Montreal Shamrock star and future Hall of Fame member declared field hockey "in its principles" is the parent of "shinny on the ice."

Hockey's Genealogy

1740 Teams of gentlemen play match of hurling on River Shannon ice near Portunna.

1769 "Shiney" reported played with wooden ball sometimes upon the ice in Scottish Highlands.

1783 Group of skaters pursue ball with hurlies on frozen New York pond.

1800 Field hockey reported played at Eton College and Royal Military College, Sandhurst, England.

1806 A game "rather like shinty" recorded as played on Albany River ice in Rupert's Land, Canada.

1813 Bandy reported played at Bury Fen, Cambridge, England.

1825 British explorer Sir John Franklin notes that members of his Northwest expedition played "hockey on the ice."

1829 "Idlers with skates on feet and hurly in hand" play 'break shins' outdoors in Nova Scotia on Sundays.

1839 First recorded games of shinty on ice at Kingston, Ontario

1842 Ricket played on Dartmouth lakes, Nova Scotia.

1843 British officers play "hockey on the ice" in Kingston, Ontario.

1844 Author claims hurley on the ice played as a boy at Windsor, Nova Scotia.

1846 Oxford student play "hockey on the ice" of Thames River.

1853 British officers and Prince Consort play "hockey on the ice" near Windsor Castle, England.

1859 Description of ricket published in Halifax, Nova Scotia: "any number of players each carrying a hurley stick."

1860 Bandy introduced to Crystal Palace,

A perfect example of "revisionist" history: An anonymous artist sketches an 1890s scene and tags it with an 1855 claim of hockey being played by the Royal Canadian Regiment in 1855.

London, England.

1862 Blackheath (field) Hockey and Football club draws up rules and regulations.

1863 Kingston-based soldiers reported playing shinny on ice.

1864 Halifax, Nova Scotia, boys play "hockey on the ice" on skates.

1867 British Garrison and Fleet play "hockey on the ice" while Dartmouth-Halifax men play ricket on the same lake ice.

1868 Eton College in Buckinghamshire, England, publishes 30 rules of (field) hockey.

1873 Quebec man claims J.G.A. Creighton of Halifax, Nova Scotia, introduced hockey (an onside game) to Montreal, Quebec.

1875 First recorded game of hockey with block of wood plays indoors in Montreal (9 aside) Creighton vs. Torrance.

1875 First (field) Hockey Association formed in London, England.

1876 Puck mentioned in Montreal game played under "Hockey Association" rules.

1876 Acadian boys play shinny-hockey at Bathurst, New Brunswick.

1877 McGill University hockey club organized in Montreal.

1877 First rules of hockey (7 in total) published in Montreal.

1877 Hockey regulations described as "Halifax

Hockey Club Rules" in Montreal.

1878 Hockey played in three 30-minutes periods (as in rugby).

1879 Hockey goal (posts 6" x 6') reported by McGill University.

1880 Seven man hockey game introduced in Montreal.

1882 Halifax Wanderers hockey club reported organized.

1882 First bandy rules drafted at St. Ives, England.

1882 Hockey introduced to Ottawa, Ontario by McGill students.

1883 Lacrosse teams play indoor hockey in Halifax (8-9 aside)

1883 First hockey trophy won by McGill at Montreal carnival.

1884 Reds and Blacks (Wanderers) defeats Blues in hockey (commonly known as hurley) in Halifax rink.

1884 Gaelic Athletic Association founded in Ireland and rules of hurling rules defined.

1885 Dartmouth builds rink; defeats Halifax Wanderers in hockey.

1886 New code of rules adopted by Amateur Hockey Association of Canada in Montreal. (Goals 4' x 6' — puck 1" x 3").

1886 Montreal teams introduce hockey to U.S.A (Burlington, Vermont)

1886 Queen's University and Royal Military College students introduce hockey to Kingston on the harbour ice.

1888 King's College-Ramblers plays hockey on Dartmouth lake. Windsor town team defeats King's College team (Windsor Skating Rink).

1889 Dartmouth Chebuctos hockey team travels to Quebec City and Montreal and plays games under Maritime (no off-sides) and Canadian (onside) rules.

1890 Ontario Hockey Association (O.H.A.) organizes at Toronto, Ontario.

1891 Ottawa Hockey Club wins first O.H.A. title.

1891 National Bandy Association founded and first rules published.

1893 Lord Stanley presents silver cup for Dominion amateur hockey championship. First recipients: Montreal A.A.A.

1895 Quebec Hockey Club plays first hockey game on artificial ice at Baltimore, Maryland.

1896 Shinty reported governed by a strict code of laws.

1898 Quebec city club proposes goal nets flush with end boards.

1899 Goal boxes introduced in Halifax game.

1900 New goal nets tested and proved in Montreal and Toronto.

J. Macdonald Oxley, a prolific children's author, wrote Standing the Test *and other stories, bringing winter and summer games to life for youths. Halifax-born, he lived and worked in Montreal, Ottawa and Toronto. He published the first comprehensive article on the history of Canadian hockey.*

References

Allen, Tom. *The Gift of the Game: A Father, a Son and the Wisdom of Hockey.* Doubleday, 2005.

Abbott, Jacob. *Caleb in Town.* Crocker, 1839.

Astley, John Dugdale. *Fifty Years of My Life.* Hurst and Blackett, 1894.

Avis, Walter S. *A Concise Dictionary of Canadianisms.* Gage, 1975.

Baker, William J. *Sports in the Western World.* Rowman and Littlefield, 1982.

Barrett, Norman. *Hockey for Men & Women.* Seeley, Service, 1955.

Beardsley, Doug. *Country on Ice.* Polestar, 1987.

Bidini, Dave. *The Best Game You Can Name.* McClelland & Stewart, 2006.

Bull, W. Perkins. *From Rattlesnake Hunt to Hockey.* Bull Foundation, 1934.

Carson, Jane. *Colonial Virginians at Play.* Colonial Williamsburg, 1989.

Culin, Stewart. *Games of North American Indians.* U.S. Government, 1907.

Dorland, Arthur G. *Former Days and Quaker Ways.* Picton Gazette, 1965.

Duff, David. *Alexandra: Princess and Queen.* Harper Collins, 1980.

Farrell, Arthur. *Hockey: Canada's Royal Winter Game.* C.R.Corneil, 1899.

Fittis, Robert Scott. *Sports and Pastimes of Scotland.* Gardner, 1891.

Fitsell, J.W. (Bill). *Hockey's Captains, Colonels & Kings.* Boston Mills Press, 1987.

Fitsell, J.W. (Bill) and Potter, Mark. *Hockey's Hub: Three Centuries of Hockey in Kingston.* Quarry Heritage Books, 2003.

Garnham, Neal. *The Oxford Companion to Irish History.* Oxford, 1998.

Goodman, Nevill and Albert. *Fen Skating.* James G. Hankin, c.1882.

Haliburton, Thomas C. *The Attache, Series II.* Richard Bentley, 1844.

Hall, Samuel Carter. *Ireland.* Jeremiah How, 1857.

Harris, Martin. *Homes of British Ice Hockey.* Tempus, 2005.

Hardy, Stephen. *The International Journal of the History of Sport.* Frank Cass, 1997.

Heller, Mark. *The Illustrated Encyclopedia of Ice Skating.* Paddington, 1979.

Hewitt, Foster. *Down the Ice.* Reginald Saunders, 1934.

Holliman, Jennie, *American Sports, 1785-1835.* Columbia University, 1931.

Jeremiah, Eddie. *Ice Hockey.* A.S. Barnes, 1942.

Jones, Martin. *Halifax-Dartmouth: Hockey's Home.* Nimbus, 2002.

King, Seamus J. *A History of Hurling.* Gill & Macmillan, 1998.

King, Seamus J. *The Clash of the Ash in Foreign Fields.* Seamus J. King, 1998.

LeSueur, Pevey. *How to Play Hockey*, 1909.

Loomer, L.S.. *Windsor, Nova Scotia: A Journey in History.* West Hants Historical Society, 1996.

Lower, Arthur M. Canada: A Country. Longmans, Green, 1948.

MacColl, Evan. *Poetical Works.* Hunter, Rose, 1885.

McKinley, Michael. *Putting a Roof on Winter.* Greystone, 2000.

Miroy, Nevil. *The History of Hockey.* Lifeline, 1986.

Moss, Peter. *Sports and Pastimes Through the Ages.* Arco, 1962.

Oxendine, Joseph B. *American Indian Sports Heritage.* Human Kinetics, 1988.

Raddall, Thomas H. *Halifax: Warden of the North.* McClelland & Stewart, 1948.

Richardson, Joanna. *Victoria and Albert.* J.M. Dent, 1977.

Rowan, John J. *The Emigrant and Sportsman in Canada.* Stanford, 1876.

Roxborough, Henry H. *One Hundred Not Out.* Ryerson, 1966.

Ryan, Dennis and Walmsley, Kevin. *Canadian Journal of Irish Studies,* 2004.

Stanley, George. *Life in the Woods.* Gesner, 1864.

Simpson, Wayne. *A Concise History of Sport in Canada.* Oxford, 1989.

Tebbutt, C.G. *The Badminton Library / Skating.* Longmans, Green, 1902.

Tomlinson, Gerald. *The Baseball Research Handbook.* SABR, 1987.

Vaughan, Garth. *The Puck Starts Here.* Goose Lane, 1996.

Withrow, W.H. *Our Own Country.* William Briggs, 1889.

Acknowledgments

The idea for this book was born ten years ago, when Ron McCulloch published *How Baseball Began: The Long Overlooked Truth about the Birth of Baseball.* The material about hockey's genesis, however, was gathered and winnowed over three decades.

Numerous researchers and writers, some of whom are long deceased, have contributed informative gems to this search. As a former reporter and editor, I like to lean heavily on quotations — the words of people on the scene, in the language of the times, when nearly every northern nation pursued a variety of stick-ball games on earth and ice.

First, I must I thank members of the Society of International Hockey Research, organized in 1991 at Kingston, Ontario, which did ice-breaking research on the game's origin. I'm especially grateful for the contributions of SIHR vice-president Edward R. Grenda, who edited the manuscript and wrote the foreword.

The resources of the International Hockey Hall of Fame and Museum and Queen's University Archives, both in Kingston, have been most beneficial to this project, as have archivists and librarians in other shrines and holdings in Ottawa, Montreal, and Halifax.

I am indebted to Neville Miroy's *History of Hockey* (Lifeline Ltd., 1986), a richly researched and astutely written story of the English field game, which has no equal in Canadian ice hockey publishing history. Seamus J. King with his *A History of Hurling* (Gill & Macmillan, 1998), deserves the same tribute. Adding to the international aspect of the story was Stephen Hardy of the University of New Hampshire and his excellent paper, sub-titled "The Making of American Ice Hockey."

Special thanks to David Battistella and Lloyd Davis for defining versions of the "rules" of the joyous game on ice, floor, or street.

The opening chapter on the contribution of native North Americans was strengthened by the letters of Jeanne L. Pattison of the McMichael Canadian Collection, and the ice polo comments compiled by Robert Levitt of the Maliseet-Micmac Institute at the University of New Brunswick, Frederiction.

The maxim, "a picture is worth a thousand words," aptly applies to the illustrations that illuminate the words of *How Hockey Happened.* The photographs and drawings were collected during vacation-research trips throughout North America and the United Kingdom. For instance, the copy of the unique painting of nineteenth-century hockey-on-the ice came through the generosity of London England's Martin C. Harris, author of *Homes of British Ice Hockey* (Tempus, 2005).

My final vote of appreciation must go to Bob Hilderley of Quarry Heritage Books, who knows the joy of playing shinny and how to balance his editing, graphic arts, and entrepreneurial skills in bringing the scintillating story of this game to the printed page.

Any omissions of the names of other people whose information and generosity have brightened these chapters are, like any errors or omissions, my responsibility alone.

This drawing of "The Hockey Player" was discovered in the British Museum in London by the late L.S. Loomer, of Wolfville, Nova Scotia, who contributed to this book. Is the ancient Roman holding a hockey stick or a scythe? The jury is still out.

Photo Credits

Author's Collection, 6, 13, 35, 40, 41, 42, 50, 61, 62, 64, 72, 84, 87, 92, 97, 102, 112, 114, 120, 124, 139, 141, 143, 147, 151
Badminton Library, 52, 55
Bettman Archives, 103
Briggs, William, 85
British Whig, 50, 136
Book of Days, 67
Boy's Own Paper, 73
Boy's Treasury, 70, 71
Broughton, Charles, 125
Brunswick Press, 5
Camanachd Association, 32
Canadian Gaelic Athletic Association, 20
Canadian Illustrated News, 91, 100
Canadian Magazine, 119
Clans of Scotland, 34
Connecticut University, 109
Corneil, C.R., 145
Currier, 39
Dominion Illustrated, 107, 140
Eastman, Seth, 11
Edwards, Frank, 95
Gilliland, Jillian Hulme , 33
Glenbow-Alberta Institute, 79, 97
Historica, iv
Harper's Young People, 81
Hewitt, Foster, 10
Hockey Review, 9
Holt, Rinehart & Winston, 60
Illustrated London News, 75
Illustrated Montreal, 38
International Bandy Federation, 54, 59
International Hockey Hall of Fame and Museum, 71, 76, 80, 101, 113, 133
King Features, 7
Kingston, City of, 131
Michael Lea/Whig-Standard, 1
LeSueur, Percy, 116
Loomer, L.S., 153
MacAlpine, Ian, Whig-Standard, 129, 131, 134
MacMillan Publishing, 31
Mansell Collection, 12
McFarlane, Brian, 142
McGill University, 78, 111
Miroy, Nevill, vii, 56, 65, 73
Montreal Daily Star, 118, 122, 123
Montreal Gazette, 121
Mullin, Willard, 25, 66
Musson Book Co., 149
National Film Board, 130
National Gallery of Art, 27
National Museum of Ireland, 19
New York Public Library, 29
Net Magazine, 30
Newark, Peter, 89
Nursery Magazine, 83
Outing, v, 151
Penny Illustrated, 89
Pigouchet's Horae ad Usum Saram, 65
Prater, Roger, 82
Public Archives Canada, 115, 117
Punch, 53, 69
Richardson, Joanna/Dent, 77
Queen's University Archives, 105
Robinson, Barry, Whig-Standard, 45
Royal Ontario Museum, 43, 93
Ryerson Press, viii, 17
St. Nicholas Magazine, 37
St. Paul's School, 99
Sports Illustrated, 57
Surry Triumphant, 90
Toronto Star, 137
Thew, Graham, 24
World Figure Skating Hall of Fame, 4
Van Verstralen, Antoni, 3
Vaughan, Garth, 15
Yale University Art Gallery, i